REFLECT

5

READING & WRITING

JESSICA WILLIAMS

Australia · Brazil · Mexico · Singapore · United Kingdom · United States

National Geographic Learning,
a Cengage Company

Reflect 5 Reading & Writing
Author: Jessica Williams

Publisher: Sherrise Roehr
Executive Editor: Laura Le Dréan
Senior Development Editor: Andrew Gitzy
Director of Global Marketing: Ian Martin
Product Marketing Manager: Tracy Baillie
Senior Content Project Manager: Mark Rzeszutek
Media Researcher: Stephanie Eenigenburg
Art Director: Brenda Carmichael
Senior Designer: Lisa Trager
Operations Coordinator: Hayley Chwazik-Gee
Manufacturing Buyer: Mary Beth Hennebury
Composition: MPS Limited

For permission to use material from this text or product,
submit all requests online at **cengage.com/permissions**
Further permissions questions can be emailed to
permissionrequest@cengage.com

Student Book ISBN: 978-0-357-44852-6
Student Book with Online Practice: 978-0-357-44858-8

National Geographic Learning
200 Pier 4 Boulevard
Boston, MA 02210

Locate your local office at **international.cengage.com/region**

Visit National Geographic Learning online at **ELTNGL.com**
Visit our corporate website at **www.cengage.com**

Printed in Mexico
Print Number: 01   Print Year: 2021

SCOPE AND SEQUENCE

WRITING	GRAMMAR	CRITICAL THINKING	REFLECT ACTIVITIES
Write a response essay	Past perfect and past perfect continuous	Apply research findings	▶ Discuss the impact of images ▶ Evaluate photographs ▶ Analyze a saying about pictures ▶ Apply research findings to your life ▶ **UNIT TASK** Write an essay in response to a photograph
Organize an essay	The passive voice	Rank factors	▶ Assess responsibility for reducing waste ▶ Analyze your contribution to a circular economy ▶ Evaluate ownership versus renting ▶ Rank factors leading to change ▶ **UNIT TASK** Write an opinion essay about an economic model
Hedge your claims	Past with *used to* and *would*	Understand hedging	▶ Consider the history of food preservation ▶ Consider how preserved foods are part of your life ▶ Consider materials in the past and present ▶ Evaluate the role of plastic in history ▶ **UNIT TASK** Write a problem-solution essay about an invention
Paraphrase original sources	Reduced non-essential adjective clauses	Apply knowledge	▶ Compare types of businesses ▶ Interpret a pie chart about businesses ▶ Relate data to a business opportunity ▶ Draw conclusions about entrepreneurs ▶ **UNIT TASK** Write an analysis essay about what makes entrepreneurs successful

WRITING	GRAMMAR	CRITICAL THINKING	REFLECT ACTIVITIES
Summarize research for a research report	Noun modifiers	Evaluate research claims	▶ Consider why we laugh ▶ Analyze different kinds of laughter ▶ Assess statements about laughter ▶ Evaluate research claims about laughter ▶ **UNIT TASK** Write a research report about laughter
Write about causes and effects	Cause and effect connectors	Be an active reader	▶ Consider how wild animals live in a city ▶ Consider a claim about cities and nature ▶ Predict how to feed our cities ▶ Assess the impact of vertical farming ▶ **UNIT TASK** Write a cause-effect essay about a change in a community
Write counterarguments and refutations	Articles	Recognize bias	▶ Rank tourist attractions ▶ Assess evidence in a travel blog ▶ Consider pros and cons of tourism ▶ Recognize bias in claims ▶ **UNIT TASK** Write an argumentative essay about the impact of tourism
Write an essay for a standardized test	Combine modals	Synthesize information from different sources	▶ Consider the role of genes in athletic performance ▶ Analyze a quote about sports ▶ Consider the impact of technology on sports ▶ Predict the future of sports records ▶ **UNIT TASK** Write an opinion essay for a standardized test

CONNECT TO IDEAS

Reflect Reading & Writing features relevant, global content to engage students while helping them acquire the academic language and skills they need. Specially-designed activities give students the opportunity to reflect on and connect ideas and language to their academic, work, and personal lives.

Academic, real-world passages invite students to explore the world while building reading skills and providing ideas for writing.

Each unit starts with a **high-interest video** to introduce the theme and generate pre-reading discussion.

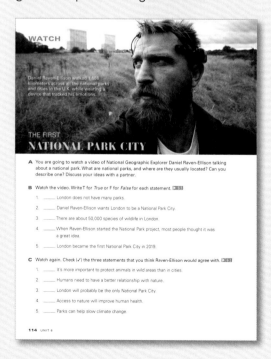

CONNECT TO ACADEMIC SKILLS

Focused **reading skills** help create confident academic readers.

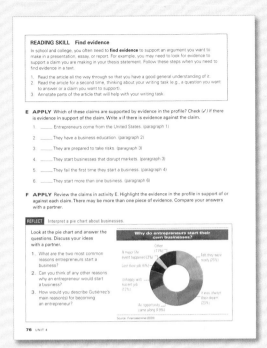

Reflect activities give students the opportunity to think critically about what they are learning and check their understanding.

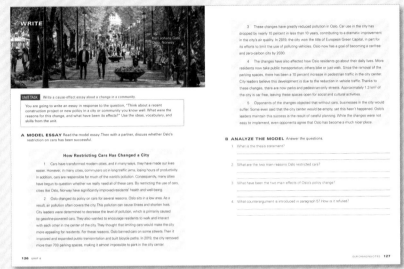

Clear writing models and analyze the model activities give students a strong framework to improve their writing.

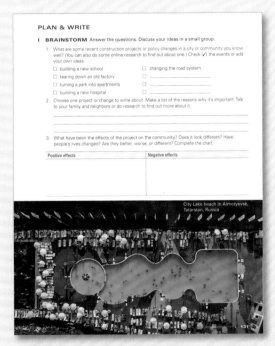

A **step-by-step approach** to the **writing process** along with relevant grammar helps students complete the final writing task with confidence.

CONNECT TO ACHIEVEMENT

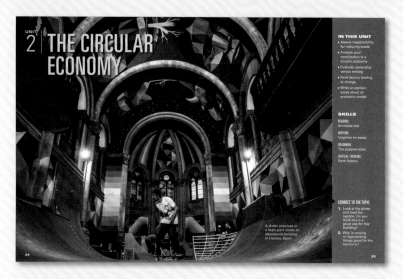

Reflect at the end of the unit is an opportunity for formative assessment. Students review the skills and vocabulary they have gained.

DIGITAL RESOURCES

TEACH lively, engaging lessons that get students to participate actively. The Classroom Presentation Tool helps teachers to present the Student's Book pages, play audio and video, and increase participation by providing a central focus for the class.

LEARN AND TRACK with Online Practice and Student's eBook. For students, the mobile-friendly platform reinforces learning through additonal and adaptive practice. For instructors, progress-tracking is made easy through the shared gradebook.

ASSESS learner performance and progress with the ExamView® Assessment Suite. For assessment, teachers create and customize tests and quizzes easily using the ExamView® Assessment Suite, available online.

ACKNOWLEDGMENTS

The Authors and Publisher would like to acknowledge the teachers around the world who participated in the development of *Reflect*.

A special thanks to our Advisory Board for their valuable input during the development of this series.

ADVISORY BOARD

Dr. Mansoor S. Almalki, Taif University, Saudi Arabia; **John Duplice**, Sophia University, Japan; **Heba Elhadary**, Gulf University for Science and Technology, Kuwait; **Hind Elyas**, Niagara College, Saudi Arabia; **Cheryl House**, ILSC Education Group, Canada; **Xiao Luo**, BFUS International, China; **Daniel L. Paller,** Kinjo Gakuin University, Japan; **Ray Purdy**, ELS Education Services, USA; **Sarah Symes,** Cambridge Street Upper School, USA.

GLOBAL REVIEWERS

ASIA

Michael Crawford, Dokkyo University, Japan; **Ronnie Hill**, RMIT University Vietnam, Vietnam; **Aaron Nurse**, Golden Path Academics, Vietnam; **Simon Park**, Zushi Kaisei, Japan; **Aunchana Punnarungsee**, Majeo University, Thailand.

LATIN AMERICA AND THE CARIBBEAN

Leandro Aguiar, inFlux, Brazil; **Sonia Albertazzi-Osorio**, Costa Rica Institute of Technology, Costa Rica; **Auricea Bacelar**, Top Seven Idiomas, Brazil; **Natalia Benavides**, Universidad de Los Andes, Colombia; **James Bonilla**, Global Language Training UK, Colombia; **Diego Bruekers Deschamp**, Inglês Express, Brazil; **Josiane da Rosa**, Hello Idiomas, Brazil; **Marcos de Campos Bueno**, It's Cool International, Brazil; **Sophia De Carvalho**, Ingles Express, Brazil; **André Luiz dos Santos**, IFG, Brazil; **Oscar Gomez-Delgado**, Universidad de los Andes, Colombia; **Ruth Elizabeth Hibas**, Inglês Express, Brazil; **Rebecca Ashley Hibas**, Inglês Express, Brazil; **Cecibel Juliao**, UDELAS University, Panama; **Rosa Awilda López Fernández**, School of Languages UNAPEC University, Dominican Republic; **Isabella Magalhães**, Fluent English Pouso Alegre, Brazil; **Gabrielle Marchetti**, Teacher's House, Brazil; **Sabine Mary**, INTEC, Dominican Republic; **Miryam Morron**, Corporación Universitaria Americana, Colombia; **Mary Ruth Popov**, Ingles Express, Ltda., Brazil; **Leticia Rodrigues Resende**, Brazil; **Margaret Simons**, English Center, Brazil.

MIDDLE EAST

Abubaker Alhitty, University of Bahrain, Bahrain; **Jawaria Iqbal**, Saudi Arabia; **Rana Khan**, Algonquin College, Kuwait; **Mick King**, Community College of Qatar, Qatar; **Seema Jaisimha Terry**, German University of Technology, Oman.

USA AND CANADA

Thomas Becskehazy, Arizona State University, AZ; **Robert Bushong**, University of Delaware, DE; **Ashley Fifer**, Nassau Community College, NY; **Sarah Arva Grosik**, University of Pennsylvania, PA; **Carolyn Ho**, Lone Star College-CyFair, TX; **Zachary Johnsrud**, Norquest College, Canada; **Caitlin King**, IUPUI, IN; **Andrea Murau Haraway**, Global Launch / Arizona State University, AZ; **Bobbi Plante**, Manitoba Institute of Trades and Technology, Canada; **Michael Schwartz**, St. Cloud State University, MN; **Pamela Smart-Smith**, Virginia Tech, VA; **Kelly Smith**, English Language Institute, UCSD Extension, CA; **Karen Vallejo**, University of California, CA.

UNIT
1 | PHOTO STORIES

Arnie, a European starling, lives with Lloyd Buck in Somerset, England.

CONNECT TO THE TOPIC

1. What do you think is going on in the photo? How does it make you feel or react?

2. What kinds of photos do you like to take?

THE PHOTOGRAPHERS ON PHOTOGRAPHY

Every spring, the Grüner See (Green Lake) in Austria floods the surrounding area, creating an underwater park.

A PREVIEW What qualities do you think someone needs to be a good photographer?

B You are going to watch a video about National Geographic photographers. As you watch, check (✓) the topics that they talk about. ▶1.1

1. _____ What their goals are
2. _____ How they began their careers
3. _____ Their passion for photography
4. _____ What they have learned in their job

5. _____ Their favorite photographs
6. _____ Advice for future photographers
7. _____ Why photos are important
8. _____ The future of photography

C Watch the first part of the video again. Complete the phrases from the video using the words in the box. ▶1.1

history	life	people	time	the world

Photos have the power to . . .

1. undo your assumptions about _____.

2. change your perspective on _____.

3. stop _____ for a moment.

4. change the course of _____.

5. make connections between _____.

PREPARE TO READ

A VOCABULARY Match the words with the definitions. Use a dictionary if necessary.

1. _____ course (of events) (n)
2. _____ deliberately (adv)
3. _____ engage (v)
4. _____ formal (adj)
5. _____ habitat (n)
6. _____ humanity (n)
7. _____ link (n)
8. _____ portrait (n)
9. _____ prompt (v)
10. _____ remote (adj)

a. a picture or photo of a person
b. a place where an animal normally lives
c. far away from other places
d. human beings as a group
e. not by accident; on purpose
f. one connection in a series
g. progress over time
h. serious; official
i. to cause something to happen
j. to hold people's attention

B Complete the paragraph with the correct form of the words. One word is extra.

engage	habitat	link	portrait	prompt	remote

Art galleries often have photography exhibits. Which types of photos are most likely to ¹_____ visitors? ²_____ of famous people usually ³_____ the strongest responses from the public. Photos of rare animals from ⁴_____ areas of the world in their natural ⁵_____ are also very popular.

C PERSONALIZE Discuss these questions with a partner.

1. What kinds of photos **engage** you the most? **Portraits**? Landscapes? Action shots?
2. Do you think that photos or videos are more likely to **prompt** an emotional response? Explain.
3. Over the **course** of your life so far, how many photos do you think you've taken?

REFLECT   Discuss the impact of images.

You are going to read about how photos can affect us. How might each of the photos described below make you feel? Write your answers in your notebook. Then discuss your ideas with a partner.

A photo of . . .

▸ a baby laughing in a father's arms
▸ an animal trapped in a cage
▸ a rock climber on the side of a mountain

▸ a frightened, lost child
▸ Earth from space
▸ a teenager helping someone elderly

VISUAL STORYTELLERS

A PREDICT Read the title and look at the photos. What kind of stories do you think the photographers are trying to tell?

🎧 1.1

1   Stories are a powerful form of communication. We use them to make sense of the world, to share our emotions, and to teach others. Visual storytelling is especially effective because images can have a powerful impact on our emotions. Photographers catch a moment that they hope will **engage** their viewers. Photographer Renée Byer says, "In this fast-paced world, . . . a still[1] photograph stops time. It gives the viewer a moment to think, to react, to feel."

2   Two National Geographic photographers—Joel Sartore and Rubén Salgado Escudero—approach visual storytelling in different ways. They use a range of techniques to tell stories through their photos. Sartore has been photographing animals for more than 25 years in an effort to raise public awareness about them. Salgado Escudero uses photos to make human connections across the world.

3   Joel Sartore began his career photographing endangered species in their natural **habitat**. He hoped that his photos would inspire people and governments to care about these animals. After several years, he changed his approach and started a new project called Photo Ark, with the goal to photograph all the animals in our world's zoos and aquariums. Instead of photographing the animals in their habitats, he began taking their **portraits**. A portrait is a very **formal** type of painting or photo. It is usually of a person standing or sitting alone, against a plain background. But Sartore started to use this technique with animals. Some of the portraits are funny, some are sad, but in most of them, the animals look straight out at us. And we look into their eyes. This technique captures the eye contact of the animals, making the animals seem almost human. Sartore does this **deliberately**, knowing that when animals look human, they are likely to **prompt** a powerful emotional response. He wants the public to fall in love with these animals, to connect with them, and to care about them. Sartore considers each animal equally important. When he photographs small animals, such as insects and frogs, he makes them look as big as a tiger. He wants to give each endangered animal an equal voice.

4   Sartore's goal is not simply to create a set of beautiful photos; he wants the Photo Ark to change viewers' minds and behavior. The disappearance of an insect or a frog may not seem very important, but every animal is an important **link** in nature. Sartore says we should not "think that we can destroy one species . . . after another and not affect **humanity**. When we save species, we're actually saving ourselves." He hopes that the Photo Ark will allow each animal to tell its story. And he hopes that these stories will convince people to make better choices about how and where they live, what they eat and wear, and how they spend their money. For example, he once photographed a group of injured koala bears. They were injured because people had moved into their habitat, and as a result, the koalas were living too close to cars and dogs. Soon after the photo was published, the government passed a law to protect the koalas.

---

[1]**still** (adj) not moving

Joel Sartore's photo of a grizzled tree-kangaroo, which is found in the rainforests of New Guinea

5   Rubén Salgado Escudero photographs people all over the world. He believes in the power of these images to make people curious and to show our shared humanity. He says that through an image we can "connect with that person or that topic even if they're thousands of miles away and have nothing to do with your reality and your world." One of his most well-known projects is the *Solar Portraits*. He traveled to **remote** communities in Myanmar, Uganda, and India. There, he took photos of people who had only recently gained access to electricity from solar-powered[2] light bulbs. He asked them to explain how that access had affected their lives. Then he set up and photographed scenes, lighted only by their solar-powered light bulbs, to show their answers. Some parents reported that the lights allowed their children to do homework in the evening. Others told him that they could now play games in the evenings. When viewers see these images, they can see that the hopes, interests, and activities of the people in these remote areas are not so different from their own.

6   Photos can tell great stories that have the power to inspire you or make you laugh or cry. In a few seconds, they can show you something you have never seen and connect you to the rest of the world. A single image can change the way you feel, think, and even push you to change your behavior. National Geographic photographer Lynn Johnson says that images are so powerful that "they can change the **course** of people's lives; they can change the course of history."

---

[2]**solar-powered** (adj) getting energy from the sun

Rubén Salgado Escudero's photo of two men working on a motorcycle by solar light, Nbeeda, Uganda

READING SKILL   Distinguish main ideas, supporting ideas, and details

It is important to understand how main ideas, supporting ideas, and details are connected in a paragraph.

The **main idea** is the most important idea and controls the content of the paragraph. It is often stated in the first or second sentence, but sometimes it is not stated at all. In this case, you have to infer—or guess—the main idea based on all the information in the paragraph.

▸ Each paragraph includes several **supporting ideas**. These support the main idea.

▸ The writer may also give **details**, such as quotes, reasons, examples, explanations, or research results, that provide evidence for the supporting ideas.

Recognizing how these three levels of information are related will improve your reading comprehension.

B MAIN IDEAS Write the correct paragraph number (3–5) for each main idea. Then write if the main idea is in the first sentence (1), is in the second sentence (2), or must be inferred (I).

Main idea	Paragraph number	1, 2, or inferred?
1. Salgado Escudero believes that photographs can bring people closer together.		
2. Sartore uses several techniques to affect viewers' emotions.		
3. Sartore believes that good photographs can lead to change.		

C DETAILS Complete the outline with supporting ideas and details. Use one or two words from the article for each answer.

I. Sartore uses techniques to affect viewers' emotions. (paragraph 3)

   A. He takes [1]_____ of animals that look directly into the viewers'

    [2]_____.

      1. This technique makes the animals look nearly [3]_____.

      2. This technique causes a(n) [4]_____.

   B. His photos make even small animals look [5]_____.

      1. This technique gives all animals a(n) [6]_____.

II. Sartore believes good photographs can lead to change. (paragraph 4)

   A. He believes saving every [7]_____ is important for our own future.

      1. "When we save species, we're actually saving [8]_____."

   B. He hopes that his pictures will persuade people to make [9]_____.

      1. His photograph of [10]_____ koalas prompted the government to change

      the [11]_____ in order to protect them.

D **DETAILS** Which of these types of details can you find in paragraph 5 of the article, *Visual Storytellers*? Find, highlight, and label the types of details with the corresponding letter.

a. quote   b. reason   c. example   d. research finding

REFLECT Evaluate photographs.

Look at these two photos. Answer the questions in your notebook. Then compare your responses in a small group.

1. What emotional responses do you have to each photo?
2. Do you think the photos are successful at telling a "visual story"? Explain.

PREPARE TO READ

A VOCABULARY Complete the sentences with the words. Use a dictionary if necessary.

assemble (v)	exclusively (adv)	mode (n)	slightly (adv)	superior (adj)
demonstrate (v)	implications (n)	recall (v)	store (v)	trigger (v)

1. Texting is not always the best _____ of communication.

2. Workers _____ hundreds of parts in a factory to make a car.

3. Most people cannot _____ events from before they were three years old.

4. Many people _____ their old photographs in boxes.

5. Old family photographs can often _____ memories of childhood.

6. Recent research has _____ for how we use our phones. It suggests that we shouldn't use them at night.

7. The experiment showed that photos are _____ to videos in engaging viewer attention. This result surprised many who believe in the power of video.

8. New smart phones are often _____ bigger than the old ones but not much bigger.

9. Some studies focus _____ on children; no adults are included.

10. Experiments _____ that adult brains are very different from children's brains.

B PERSONALIZE Discuss these questions with a partner.

1. How do you **store** your favorite photographs? In a photo album? In the cloud?
2. What are the **implications** of having only digital copies of photographs?
3. What was the last thing you had to **assemble**? How easy was it to assemble?

REFLECT Analyze a saying about pictures.

You are going to read about how our brain processes images. Before you read, discuss these questions in a small group.

1. What do you think the expression "A picture is worth a thousand words" means?
2. Why do you think we have a stronger response to pictures than to words?

OUR VISUAL BRAIN

A PREDICT Read the title and look at the photo and Figure 1. What do you think the reading will be mostly about?

a. A discussion of where the brain stores images during reading

b. A comparison of how the brain responds to images and text

c. An explanation of how our visual abilities have evolved

A family in New Mexico, USA, looks at old family photos.

🎧 1.2

1   You've probably heard the saying, "A picture is worth a thousand words." But have you thought about why that might be the case? We can read, write, and use advanced technology, so why is a simple image often more powerful than printed words on a page? The answer lies in our brains. The brain has a strong emotional response to images. In addition, the brain can process images very quickly and **store** a large number of them as memories. It's all part of what it means to be human.

2   A picture can be a more effective **mode** of communication than words to tell a story. It is more likely than text to **trigger** an emotional response, and strong emotions are more likely to lead to action or changes in behavior. Imagine that you hear about people suffering in a war zone or after a natural disaster. You are more likely to do something to help those people if you see a picture than if you read about them. In addition, scientific studies have shown that we remember those powerful emotions for a long time. This is true even if you see the image for less than a second.

3   Images have other effects on memory as well. Humans are able to store a huge number of images, and they can remember those images in detail. In one study, participants saw 2,500 different images. Later, they looked at another set of images. Some of these images were exactly the same as the previous images, and some were **slightly** different. Participants had to decide if the images in the second set were the same or different from the ones they had already seen. They were able to do this correctly 90 percent of the time. Images also improve your memory of written text. If you see a word and image together, you are more likely to remember the word. This effect was **demonstrated** in a study in which participants were able to **recall** only 10 percent of words presented alone. However, when they saw a word with a picture (e.g., the word *fork* with a picture of a fork), they were able to recall 65 percent of them.

4   Our emotional response to images may be one explanation for their impact on memory. But scientists believe there may be a second reason: how images are stored in the brain. Information about images is stored in two places. In one place, the information is stored as the image, and in another place, it is stored as a *label* for the image. In other words, there is a picture of an elephant in one part of your brain, and the label "elephant" in another. This process is called *dual encoding*, and it creates strong memories.

5   Speed is still another advantage that images have over text. The brain can process a whole image very quickly—in less than a second. It can process more than a thousand images in a minute. Compare this to the average reading speed of 200–250 words per minute. Why is reading so slow? The brain processes each letter, or other written symbol in a word, as a little image. Then it **assembles** the letters as words and the words as sentences. All of this takes a long time. This difference between how the brain responds to images and written text is called the Picture Superiority Effect (see Figure 1), and it explains why our memory of images is **superior** to our memory of text.

6   The Picture Superiority Effect has wide **implications**. Today, social media relies increasingly on visual information and with good reason. A recent study found that posts were 94 percent more likely to be reposted if they included an image. The fastest-growing social media platforms are visual, for example, Pinterest and Instagram. Facebook is also increasingly visual. Posts with still[1] images have the highest level of user interaction, such as liking, reposting, and responding. This is higher than text alone or even videos. Still images are also an essential part of advertising. A photograph tells customers how a product looks, but it can also help them imagine how that product would fit into their lives. "How would that carpet look on my floor?" "I can see myself in that car." Businesses know that customers who see images of products are more likely to buy them. Some companies rely almost **exclusively** on photographs in their advertisements. For example, most Apple advertisements include just the name and a photograph of the product. The picture tells the whole story.

7   The human brain is uniquely evolved to process visual information. This gives photographs the power to tell stories with deep and lasting impact, everywhere from the news, to social media, to advertising.

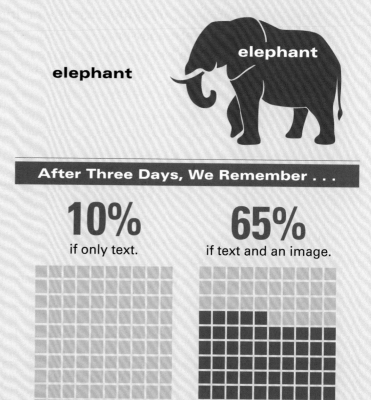

Figure 1. The Picture Superiority Effect

---

[1]**still** (adj) not moving

B MAIN IDEAS Write the correct paragraph number (2–6) next to its main idea. Two ideas are extra.

a. _____ Images affect our memories more than text.

b. _____ The effects of picture superiority can be seen in many different areas.

c. _____ Evolutionary processes can explain the superiority of images.

d. _____ A photo can prompt powerful emotions that often result in action.

e. _____ Images and texts are stored in different ways in the brain.

f. _____ Images can help us understand written text better and more quickly.

g. _____ The brain processes images more quickly than words.

C DETAILS Complete the sentences. Use no more than three words or numbers from the article for each answer.

1. Participants could tell if the images were different _____ of the time. (paragraph 3)

2. Participants remembered _____ of words without pictures. (paragraph 3)

3. Our brain stores images and text in separate places—a process called _____. (paragraph 4)

4. In a minute, people can process over _____ pictures. (paragraph 5)

5. Our brain responds better to images because of a concept called the _____. (paragraph 5)

6. There is a greater possiblity that a customer will _____ a product when he or she sees images of it. (paragraph 6)

D DETAILS Choose the type of detail for each sentence in activity C.

1. a. explanation   b. example   c. research finding
2. a. quote   b. reason   c. research finding
3. a. example   b. explanation   c. reason
4. a. quote   b. reason   c. statistic
5. a. example   b. explanation   c. research finding
6. a. example   b. reason   c. statistic

CRITICAL THINKING   Apply research findings

Many academic articles include findings from scientific research. When you read about research, think about how the findings could apply to other areas of your life. For example, consider the research included in *Our Visual Brain*. If you wanted to convince people to help wild animals, would you use photos or a newspaper article?

REFLECT   Apply research findings to your life.

How could the Picture Superiority Effect help you in your life? Consider the areas below. Write notes in your notebook. Then discuss them with a partner.

schoolwork   in a job   shopping online   using social media

WRITE

UNIT TASK Write an essay in response to a photograph.

You are going to write a response essay about a photograph that makes or made you think or act differently. Use the ideas, vocabulary, and skills from the unit.

A MODEL Look at the photo. Then read the model essay. Why did the writer have such a strong reaction to the photo? Highlight the sentence that gives the reason for her response.

Paradise Lost?

1   We've all heard the expression "A picture is worth a thousand words," but do people really believe it? I didn't, not until I saw the photograph. I had read about this problem for years, but that wasn't the same as the photo. I never thought I would say this, but a photograph made me make some changes in my life.

2   The photo showed a beach in Bali, Indonesia. I had been to that beach four times. It was the most beautiful place in the world. For me, it was a remote paradise with clean white sand and clear blue water. But this didn't show any of that. Instead, it showed a beach covered in plastic—plastic bags, plastic cups, plastic boxes—as well as dead fish and other animals. I had read about the problem of garbage washing up on islands across the Pacific and Indian Oceans. I had heard news reports about huge amounts of plastic floating in the ocean, but the photo made the situation real for me.

3   Looking at the photo broke my heart because the beach was such a special memory for me. The photo sat on my kitchen table for days. I looked at it and then at my vacation photos on the wall. I was so disappointed in the tourists who visited but did not respect this lovely place. I was angry at the people all over the world who threw away plastic items without thinking. How could I help? I certainly couldn't go back to Bali to help clean up the beach. I thought to myself, "I recycle—isn't that enough?" Looking at the photograph again, I knew the answer to that question was clearly, "no."

4   After I did some research and thought about the problem for a while, I decided I had to take a first step, even though it was a small one. When I looked closely at the photograph, I could see that many of the plastic items were related to food. I had already been recycling plastic for years, but I wanted to cut plastic out completely from my food preparation and

A beach near the village of Jimbaran, Bali, Indonesia

storage. So, I stopped using plastic bags. Now, I take small reusable bags to the supermarket. I use them for fruits and vegetables. I put leftover food in bowls or pots with lids. I never wrap anything in plastic. I keep a coffee cup, plates, forks, and knives in my desk at my office, and I wash them after I use them. I even have a metal straw!

5 Every day I am learning new ways to reduce my use of plastic. I know it is just a small step by one person, but I hope it will make a difference. I should have done this a long time ago, but I'm glad I have that photograph that prompted me to make changes in my life.

B ANALYZE THE MODEL Write the correct paragraph number (1–5) next to its purpose.

a. _____ Describes the photograph

b. _____ Shows what the writer has learned

c. _____ Describes how the writer's behavior changed in response to the photo

d. _____ Catches readers' attention

e. _____ Describes the writer's feelings in response to the photo

WRITING SKILL   Write a response essay

In a personal response essay, you write about your reaction to something that you have seen, read, or heard. You can organize your personal response essay in the following way.

▸ Introductory paragraph: Include a **hook** at the beginning—a sentence that draws readers in and makes them want to know what comes next. Finish the introductory paragraph with a **thesis statement** that tells the reader what to expect in the essay. Avoid using statements such as: *I am going to tell you how I feel about this.*

▸ First body paragraph: Describe what you are responding to—a photo, a painting, a song, etc. Provide details.

▸ Second body paragraph: Describe your emotional response. Provide details.

▸ Third body paragraph: Describe how your life changed. How did you think or act differently? Provide details.

▸ Concluding paragraph: Say what you learned or what you will do next.

C APPLY Underline the hook in the model essay. Highlight the thesis statement.

D APPLY Choose the two best thesis statements for a response essay. Discuss your reasons with a partner.

  a. After reading the article, I knew I had to learn more about the culture of Japan.

  b. I liked the photo a lot because it had very beautiful flowers.

  c. Let me tell you my opinion of this image.

  d. This film opened my eyes to the importance of climate change.

  e. I recommend that you go see this exhibit before it travels to another city.

E APPLY Choose the three best hooks for a response essay. Discuss your reasons with a partner.

  a. Do you know how big a great white shark is? I recently found out—in a very unusual way.

  b. I had been looking at the photo for hours when suddenly the idea came to me.

  c. The concert at the city arena last night was amazing, and my friends and I all enjoyed it.

  d. The movie theater was so cold that I could not feel my fingers, but I had to see how the film ended.

  e. The plot of this book was not very interesting, and the main character was boring.

F APPLY Choose a photo in the unit. In your notebook, write some words or phrases about how the photo makes you feel. Then write a paragraph to describe it.

A SpaceX Falcon rocket launching at Cape Canaveral, Florida, USA

G NOTICE THE GRAMMAR Review the verbs in paragraph 2 of the model essay. Underline the actions or events that happened before the author saw the photo. Discuss your answers with a partner.

GRAMMAR   Past perfect and past perfect continuous

The past perfect and past perfect continuous show actions and events that happen before other past actions or events. The past perfect helps make the order of two past events clear.

> Sartore **had taken** thousands of photos of animals in their natural habitat
> 1st
> but then <u>decided</u> to take portraits instead.
> 2nd

The past perfect and past perfect continuous can provide background information or explanations for events and actions that happen later.

> The woman in the photo <u>was smiling</u> because she **had** just **received** good news.

The past perfect is often used in relation to specific past times and events (e.g., *by Monday, since he was a child*) and with time words (e.g., *already, never*).

> She **had visited Bali** several times <u>before the tsunami</u>.

The past perfect continuous emphasizes a continuous state or activity, often in contrast to another past event that interrupts it.

> Rubén Salgado Escudero **had been working** in the video game industry for ten years <u>when he started</u> taking pictures.

H GRAMMAR Complete the sentences with the correct form of the verb in parentheses. Use the past perfect or past perfect continuous for ONE of the verbs in each sentence.

1. Because I _____ (study) photography in school, I _____ (be) able to get a job on the staff of the local newspaper.

2. The tourists _____ (hope) to see the exhibition of famous portraits, but when they _____ (arrive) it was too late, and the museum was already closed.

3. We _____ (be) disappointed because we _____ (wait) more than an hour for a chance to talk to the photographer. Unfortunately, he _____ (leave) without answering any questions.

4. She was happy when she _____ (receive) an offer from National Geographic because she _____ (look) for a job as a wildlife photographer for more than a year.

5. The study participants _____ (remember) more than half of the images they _____ (see) the day before.

6. When the research study finally _____ (end), the participants _____ (describe) more than a thousand images.

I EDIT Find and correct six errors with the past perfect and past perfect continuous.

A Change of Heart

By the time my friend Gabriela was 18, she studied drawing for more than 10 years. She was always drawing pictures of her friends and family. She wanted to be a painter. She loved art since she was very small, but after she started college, she started to question her goals. Then, one day, a friend invited her to an art gallery to see a photography exhibit. She never really looked at photographs as art until that moment. Looking at the photos in the gallery was a completely new experience. Every photo had told a story. When she went home that night, she realized that she studied the wrong thing. She loved art, but she decided that she wanted to study photography. The next week she changed her major to photography.

After that, in addition to taking courses, she worked as a photographer for the college newspaper. She learned everything she could. Three years later, she graduated. She got a great job with a magazine. She traveled all over the world taking photographs. By the time she was 30, she traveled to all seven continents, including Antarctica! She has been very happy and knows that she made the right decision.

PLAN & WRITE

J BRAINSTORM Think about photos that you know well. Choose a photo that made or makes you think or act differently. Write notes about the photo.

1. What does the photo show? Where was it taken?

    _____

    _____

2. What story is the photo trying to tell? How does it tell this story?

    _____

    _____

3. Why did/does this photo interest you?

    _____

    _____

4. How did/does the photo make you feel or react?

    _____

    _____

5. What did/does the photo inspire you to do or learn?

    _____

    _____

A weather emergency in Venice, Italy

K OUTLINE Complete the outline for your essay.

Introductory paragraph Hook: _____

_____

Thesis statement: _____

_____

First body paragraph The photo shows _____

_____

Supporting ideas/Details: _____

_____

Second body paragraph When I looked at the photo, I felt _____

_____

Supporting ideas/Details: _____

_____

Third body paragraph After looking at the photo for a while, I decided _____

_____

Supporting ideas/Details: _____

_____

Concluding paragraph From this photo, I learned _____

_____

L FIRST DRAFT Use your outline to write a first draft of your essay.

M REVISE Use this list as you write your second draft.
- ☐ Does your hook catch the reader's attention?
- ☐ Does your thesis statement tell readers what will be in your response?
- ☐ Does your first body paragraph describe the photograph?
- ☐ Does your second body paragraph describe how you felt or reacted?
- ☐ Does your third body paragraph explain how you changed or responded?
- ☐ Does your concluding paragraph show what you learned or what you plan to do?

N EDIT Use this list as you write your final draft.
- ☐ Did you use the past perfect and past perfect continuous correctly?
- ☐ Do your subjects and verbs agree?
- ☐ Did you spell all the words correctly?

O FINAL DRAFT Reread your final draft and correct any errors. Then submit it to your teacher.

REFLECT

A Check (✓) the Reflect activities you can do and the academic skills you can use.

- ☐ discuss the impact of images
- ☐ evaluate photographs
- ☐ analyze a saying about pictures
- ☐ apply research findings to your life
- ☐ write an essay in response to a photograph
- ☐ distinguish main ideas, supporting ideas, and details
- ☐ write a response essay
- ☐ past perfect and past perfect continuous
- ☐ apply research findings

B Write the vocabulary words from the unit in the correct column. Add any other words that you learned. Circle words you still need to practice.

NOUN	VERB	ADJECTIVE	ADVERB & OTHER

C Reflect on the ideas in the unit as you answer these questions.

1. What is the most important thing you learned in this unit?

_____

_____

2. Do you think you will use images more often now? At school, at work, or on social media?

_____

_____

THE CIRCULAR ECONOMY

A skater practices in a skate park inside an abandoned building in Llanera, Spain.

CONNECT TO THE TOPIC

1. Look at the photo and read the caption. Do you think this is a good use for this building?

2. Why is reusing or repurposing things good for the economy?

WATCH

A NATURAL CYCLE

Plitvice Lakes National Park, Croatia

A PREDICT You are going to watch a video about linear and circular economies. How do you think the two economies are different?

B Watch the video. Read the statements. Check (✓) the three statements that are true for each type of economy. ▷ 2.1

Linear economy

1. _____ There is no waste.

2. _____ When a plant or animal dies, it goes back into the ground.

3. _____ When something is old or breaks, we throw it away.

4. _____ The system works in a never-ending circle.

5. _____ Unhealthy waste is produced.

6. _____ Energy comes from the sun.

7. _____ Valuable resources are reduced.

Circular economy

1. _____ Materials are made from natural resources that can be easily recycled.

2. _____ People buy less stuff.

3. _____ People need to replace their phones and devices more often.

4. _____ Products are designed to make it easier to reuse valuable parts.

5. _____ It is similar to the biological cycle in nature.

PREPARE TO READ

A VOCABULARY Read the sentences. Choose the correct meaning for the words in bold.

1. A lot of people **claim** that they recycle, but the evidence is that they do not.

   a. believe   b. make a promise   c. say something is true

2. The team **collaborated** to create the highest quality product. Each member did a great job.

   a. worked together b. competed   c. designed

3. The **components** of a laptop, which are made in different countries, are put together in a factory.

   a. ideas   b. parts   c. data

4. We cannot **eliminate** all our problems, but we can reduce the number of them.

   a. end completely b. find the cause of   c. survive

5. Energy companies **extract** raw materials from the earth to make oil and steel.

   a. sell   b. take out   c. locate

6. Manufacturers throw away products that have **flaws** because consumers won't buy products that aren't perfect.

   a. owners   b. holes   c. mistakes

7. Humans should live in **harmony** with nature. It is healthier for them and the environment.

   a. collection   b. natural protection   c. peaceful cooperation

8. One **principle** of economics is that consumers buy less when prices go up.

   a. basic rule   b. relationship   c. popular idea

9. Working 16 hours a day, 6 days a week is not a **sustainable** way to live.

   a. able to help   b. profitable   c. able to last a long time

10. Unfortunately, shoes **wear out** quickly if you use them every day.

    a. become damaged b. become more   c. become dirty
      or useless   comfortable

REFLECT Assess responsibility for reducing waste.

You are going to read about how the circular economy can reduce waste. Who do you think has the greatest responsibility for reducing waste? Discuss your answers with a partner.

▸ Charities
▸ Individual people
▸ International organizations
▸ Local communities

▸ National governments
▸ Specific industries or companies
▸ Other: _____

CLOSING THE
CIRCLE ON WASTE

A PREVIEW Look at Figure 1. Do you think we live in a linear economy, a circular economy, or a combination of both?

Clearas, a company in Missoula, Montana, USA, uses algae to clean wastewater.

1   Each year, we take more than 100 billion tons of raw material from the earth—including rock, minerals, and fossil fuels—to make many of the products we buy. About two-thirds of this raw material eventually becomes waste. Much of that waste comes from products that we throw away, including almost 3 billion plastic bottles that end up in the ocean and 1.5 billion tires that end up in landfills[1] every year. This waste is an economic design **flaw**.

2   For centuries, we have followed a model called the *linear economy*. Industries take raw materials, they make things, we use them, and then we throw them away. Environmentalists and economists warn that this model is not **sustainable**. They have proposed an alternative: a *circular economy*.

3   A circular economy is based on the idea of **eliminating** waste by keeping raw materials and products in use for much longer. It works in a circle, very much the way nature does. The circular economy uses a range of strategies. Some of them, such as recycling, are familiar; others, such as refurbishing, may be less familiar. The circular economy brings us back into **harmony** with nature.

Two economic models

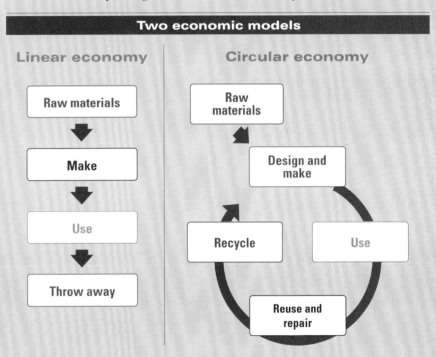

Figure 1

4   In a circular economy, products are designed from the beginning to be long-lasting and easy to repair. This means that products are made from higher-quality materials. It also means that devices, such as phones and computers, are designed so that their parts are easy to access. These steps reduce the need for new raw materials. One example

[1]**landfill** (n) a place where trash is buried

of this is the shoe company Timberland. They wanted to produce shoes that use less raw material. So, they **collaborated** with a tire manufacturer in Singapore. The company agreed to make tires with the high-quality rubber that Timberland needs for their shoes. When the tires **wear out**, their rubber is recycled as shoe soles[2], reducing Timberland's need for new rubber.

5   In a linear economy, consumers throw away products when they wear out, but this is less likely to happen in a circular economy. Because better-designed products last longer, they can be used again and again. If one user no longer wants a product, it can go back to the manufacturer for refurbishing. In the refurbishing process, broken, torn, or worn-out parts are replaced or repaired. A refurbished product is often almost as good as new. This refurbished product can then be sold to another customer.

6   Of course, nothing lasts forever, so it's also important to consider what happens when a product can no longer be used, repaired, or refurbished. This is part of another important strategy in a circular economy—recycling. Valuable **components** are **extracted** from products for reuse in a new or different product. For example, electronic products contain a range of components, many of which are valuable and can be recycled. It is estimated that there is $62.5 billion worth of valuable metals, including gold, silver, and copper, in the electronic devices in use today. Yet, only about 20 percent of electronics are recycled; instead, most of them become part of the 50 million tons of annual e-waste.

But that's starting to change. Since 2001, Japanese law has required manufacturers of televisions and home appliances, such as washing machines, to collect and recycle their products. The cost is shared by the manufacturer, consumers, and the government. In other countries, individual businesses are taking the lead. Apple, for example, encourages customers to trade in old iPhones. Robots then take them apart and extract materials for new devices.

7   A basic **principle** of the circular economy is that any waste should be used to make another product. For the food industry, dealing with waste is an important concern. One trillion dollars of food goes to waste every year. But a company in the U.K., Entocycle, is using some of it in an unusual way—to grow black flies. Flies eat just about anything; they love food waste. They eat the waste, then lay eggs, and the eggs hatch into larvae[3], which are an excellent source of protein. Entocycle sells the larvae to fish farms. There it is fed to the salmon that will end up on our dining tables. This is a good example of a perfect economic circle.

8   Some critics of the circular economy **claim** it will hurt businesses, but supporters argue the opposite. They believe that it will create opportunities for new types of businesses. One recent study suggests that moving to a circular economy could add $2 trillion to the global economy by 2050.

---

[2]**sole** (n) the bottom of a shoe

[3]**larvae** (n pl) the young form of insects, such as flies or butterflies

Entocycle is an insect-farming company in London, UK.

B MAIN IDEAS Write the correct paragraph number (2–8) next to its main idea.
One idea is extra.

a. _____ The waste from one product can be used to make something else.

b. _____ Some countries are able to reuse or recycle all of their waste.

c. _____ The goal of a circular economy is to use resources responsibly and eliminate waste.

d. _____ The circular economy is good for the environment but also good for business.

e. _____ Valuable components can be extracted and recycled after products wear out.

f. _____ Improved design can extend a product's life and reduce the use of raw materials.

g. _____ Products with good design can be refurbished more easily.

h. _____ The linear economy model has been followed for a long time.

C DETAILS Write the terms next to the correct examples.

component	e-waste	raw materials	recycling	refurbishing

1. _____ an old laptop that is in a landfill

2. _____ removing some metal from an old television and using it in a new smartphone

3. _____ repairing or replacing parts in an old machine to make it ready for another customer

4. _____ copper, rubber, or sand

5. _____ the copper wiring inside a smartphone

D DETAILS Read the statements. Write T for *True* or F for *False* based on the information in the article. Then correct the false statements.

1. _____ We waste about 90 percent of the raw material we take from the earth.

2. _____ Timberland is collaborating with a plastic bottle manufacturer.

3. _____ Electronics today contain about $62 billion worth of valuable metals.

4. _____ We throw away about 50 million tons of electronics every year.

5. _____ Furniture makers in Japan are required to collect and recycle their products.

6. _____ About a trillion tons of food are wasted every year.

7. _____ The circular economy could add $2 billion to the economy by 2050.

READING SKILL   Annotate text

Annotating while you read means marking important ideas in an article. This helps you remember more information from the article and makes it easier for you to answer questions about it later. Below is a common system that you can use to annotate effectively.

1. **Highlight** main ideas in one color. Remember, main ideas are often in the first or second sentence in a paragraph.
2. **Highlight** important supporting ideas and details in another color. You can add numbers in the margin to indicate the order of these ideas (*1*, *2*, *3*).
3. Underline any sentences that summarize the ideas in a paragraph or article.
4. Circle words you don't know. You can go back later and look them up.
5. Underline things you want to comment on with a **wavy line** and include **short notes** in the margin, such as:

   ▸ an example: *Ex.*
   ▸ something you agree with: *Great point!*
   ▸ something you have a question about: *?*
   ▸ information that relates to your life: *True for me!*

E APPLY Annotate the paragraph. More than one answer is possible.

Designers at the company Miniwiz have developed more than 12,000 new materials from trash, which can be used in construction. In 2013, they created an entire store made from trash. They used 5,500 soda cans, 2,000 water bottles, and 50,000 old CDs. Their most famous design is EcoARK, a temporary building made from 1.5 million plastic bottles. Miniwiz melted the plastic bottles and then made them into bricks similar to LEGO blocks. The building was nine stories tall and strong enough to withstand fires, earthquakes, and hurricanes. These are just two innovative examples of how Miniwiz is helping bring us closer to a circular economy.

F APPLY Annotate paragraphs 4 and 7 of the article, *Closing the Circle on Waste.* Then compare your annotations with a partner.

REFLECT   Analyze your contribution to a circular economy.

Look at the items below. What do you do when these items wear out or break? Do you ever repair them, recycle them, or give them to a company to refurbish? Discuss your answers in a small group.

a backpack	eyeglasses	shoes
a bicycle	a phone	headphones

PREPARE TO READ

A VOCABULARY Read the sentences. Discuss the meaning of the words in bold with a partner.

▶ The growing population has led to an increased **demand** for electricity.

▶ Regular repairs can **extend** the life span of appliances for many more years.

▶ The **key** to active reading is taking good notes.

▶ The cost of home **ownership** is increasing every year.

▶ Some people have so many **possessions** that they cannot fit all of them into their homes.

▶ Many people bring their own bags to a store to carry their **purchases**.

▶ Solar and wind power are **renewable** sources of energy. Oil and gas are not.

▶ A **survey** of Japanese adults asked about their support for a circular economy.

▶ Many people **turn to** their families first when they need financial help.

▶ A lot of people **upgrade** to the latest smartphone as soon as it's released.

B VOCABULARY Write the words from activity A next to their definitions.

1. _____ (n) a set of questions to find out what people think or do

2. _____ (n) the need for goods or services

3. _____ (adj) able to be replaced or renewed

4. _____ (v) to make something last longer

5. _____ (n) the state of owning something

6. _____ (v) to improve something or exchange it for something better

7. _____ (n) the most important thing

8. _____ (n) things that you buy

9. _____ (v phr) to get help from someone

10. _____ (n) things that you own

C PERSONALIZE Discuss these questions with a partner.

1. Do you respond to online **surveys**? Why or why not?
2. Who do you **turn to** first when you need help with technology?
3. How can you **extend** the life of your phone?

REFLECT Evaluate ownership versus renting.

Before you read about how ownership is changing, think about which of these products you would be happy renting instead of owning. Discuss your answer with a partner.

a camera	a phone	a sofa
camping equipment	shoes	a suit or dress

READ

THE RISE OF
USERSHIP

Helsinki, Finland

A PREVIEW Read the title. Answer
the questions with a partner.

1. What do you think usership means?

2. How do you think usership is
different from ownership?

🎧 2.2

1   Do you need to *own* a phone? A sofa? A car? Some people want to buy things and use them for many years. But in a circular economy, you don't have to. This is because many businesses are moving away from traditional **ownership** models of selling products. Instead, they are moving to different models that include renting their products or offering "products-as-a-service." The **key** to the success of these usership models is that products are of high quality and can be repaired or **upgraded** easily. That way, one product can have a long life and many users.

2   When people move into their first home, they often look for inexpensive furniture. Many of them **turn to** options like IKEA, the Swedish furniture company, for these **purchases**. However, some of this furniture is not designed—or expected—to last very long. When it breaks, the owners often just throw it away. In the United States alone, 12 million tons of furniture go into landfills every year. IKEA is trying to address this waste problem in several ways. First, the company has begun to rent some of its products in parts of Europe. Each time a product comes back from a renter, it is refurbished, **extending** the life of the product. Second, customers who buy new furniture can sell it back to IKEA. The company will clean it, refurbish it, then sell or rent it to a new customer. With this in mind, IKEA has started to design its products for longer life and easier repair. It is testing which parts of chairs, tables, lamps, etc. are likely to break or wear out first. Their goal is to make it possible to replace just that part, giving each piece of furniture a longer life. This model works well for products we use every day, such as furniture, but it makes even more sense for products that we use less frequently, for example, camping equipment and wedding dresses, both of which have growing rental and resale markets.

3   Renting and reselling are not the only trends away from ownership. More and more consumers are choosing to pay a monthly fee for a service that allows them to use products instead of buying them. This model—sometimes called product-as-a-service—is already popular in the music and publishing industries. It is becoming more common across a wide range of other industries, including the smartphone market. The Dutch phone company Fairphone manufactures smartphones using sustainable materials and environmentally friendly methods. But it doesn't sell its phones. Instead, customers pay a monthly fee to use them. Because the company designs high-quality phones that are easy to repair, they last a long time, and they are less likely to end up in a landfill.

4   For consumers, the benefits of usership are clear. They don't have to pay a high purchase cost or worry about maintenance. They can easily and cheaply repair or upgrade their products. Young people, in particular, are attracted to usership models. They prefer having access to products, rather than owning them. Many of them don't want the responsibility of having a lot of **possessions**.

Consumer interest in these kinds of services is increasing dramatically for everything from cars to clothing. A recent report found that sales of these kinds of services have grown over 300 percent worldwide in seven years.

5   For businesses, usership also has advantages. Fairphone's service provides the company with regular and predictable income. For IKEA, usership strategies are helping the company to plan ahead for the day when it will be harder to get the non-**renewable** raw materials needed to produce furniture. And for both Fairphone and IKEA, as well as other companies like them, moving to a usership model can improve their public image—it shows that they care about the environment. This positive public image is good for business.

6   It is likely that the move from ownership to usership will continue to expand, partly in response to growing consumer **demand** for greener[1] products. A recent **survey** of 15,000 people in Asia, Europe, and North America found that consumers are increasingly concerned about the environmental damage that waste can cause. More than half of them said they would pay a higher price to be sure that products are made in an environmentally friendly way. As the demand for environmentally friendly products and services grows, manufacturers may need to move more quickly to adapt to the end of ownership.

[1]**greener** (adj) more environmentally friendly

The Dutch company Fairphone rents its smartphones to users for a small monthly fee.

B Annotate paragraphs 4 and 5 of the article. Then compare your annotations with a partner.

C **MAIN IDEAS** Put the main ideas in the order that they appear in the article (1–6).

a. _____ The end of ownership is growing in response to consumer demand.

b. _____ One furniture company is experimenting with the usership model.

c. _____ Usership models are good for consumers.

d. _____ Businesses are moving from ownership to usership models.

e. _____ The end of ownership can also benefit businesses.

f. _____ One popular new model is "product-as-a-service."

D **DETAILS** Check (✓) the statements that are true for each company.

The company . . .	IKEA	Fairphone
1. resells used products.		
2. is designing products that last longer.		
3. is making products that are easier to repair.		
4. doesn't sell products.		
5. charges a fee for a service.		
6. is planning for a decrease in raw materials.		
7. wants to improve its public image.		

CRITICAL THINKING **Rank factors**

It can be useful to rank factors in order of importance or significance. For example, many people use email less today than 10 years ago. Why? Is it our busy schedules? A concern for privacy? A wish for more immediate communication, such as texting? Deciding how important each factor is can help you understand why something occurred or may occur. These factors may change over time, so it may be useful to reconsider your rankings occasionally.

REFLECT Rank factors leading to change.

What will push us toward a circular economy? Rank the factors in terms of their power to cause change (1–5, with 1 being most important). Then discuss your ideas in a small group.

_____ Increasing pollution

_____ Demand for environmentally friendly products

_____ Running out of raw materials

_____ International cooperation among nations

_____ Lower cost of producing environmentally friendly products

These old car parts are ready for refurbishing and recycling in A Coruña, Galicia, Spain.

UNIT TASK   Write an opinion essay about an economic model.

You are going to write an essay in response to the question, "Which economic model is more beneficial for individuals: linear or circular?" Use the ideas, vocabulary, and skills from the unit.

A MODEL Read the model essay in response to the question, "Does a circular economy benefit the environment?" Check (✓) the benefits the writer mentions.

1. _____ fewer raw materials   2. _____ less expensive   3. _____ less waste   4. _____ simpler

The Environment and the Circular Economy

1   Our planet is like a living, breathing body—a bit like our own bodies. When we treat our bodies well, we stay healthy. When we treat our bodies badly, we get sick. The "take-make-throw away" economic model is making our planet sick. This is because the "inputs" (everything we take from the earth) and the "outputs" (everything we make or throw away) are not in balance.

If we move to a circular economy, both inputs and outputs will be better balanced, so our planet will stay healthy.

2   A circular economy recycles and reuses raw materials and doesn't waste them. In contrast, a linear economy takes billions of tons of these "inputs" from the earth and reuses less than 10 percent of them. This means some critical resources such as minerals, sand, and metals could be gone forever. A circular economy, on the other hand, uses these "inputs" more responsibly. For example, products are designed to last longer, which reduces the need for new raw materials. The circular economy takes fewer resources as inputs from the planet. It also means that the resources that we do take will last longer. This is better for the planet and for our future.

3   A circular economy also reduces the number of products we throw away. One problem with the linear economy is that we waste too much of our output. A lot of this waste ends up in landfills or the ocean. In a circular economy, products are recycled, reused, repaired, and refurbished, so fewer products end up in landfills. Instead, they are used to make something else. For example, glass jars and bottles can be recycled to make building materials.

4   In a circular economy, fewer raw materials are taken from the earth, and they are used more responsibly than in a linear economy. Just as important, waste is reduced or eliminated, which decreases the harmful effects on the environment. But, in my view, we have to hurry. Time may be running out for our planet.

WRITING SKILL   Organize an essay

Most essays are structured in a similar way. The most important element is the **thesis statement**. A thesis statement includes the **topic** and the **claim** (often called the **controlling idea**) you want to make about the topic. The rest of the essay provides evidence to support your claim. There are three main parts of an essay.

▶ An **introductory paragraph** starts with a **hook** that captures readers' interest so that they will want to keep reading. The hook is often an interesting statement or question. After, you may provide some background information to explain more about the topic. The final sentence or sentences present your thesis, often called the **thesis statement**.

▶ **Body paragraphs** give evidence to support the claim in the thesis statement. Each paragraph usually starts with a main idea, called a **topic sentence**, followed by supporting ideas to develop the main idea. Details can be included, such as examples, statistics, research results, or personal experience.

▶ A **concluding paragraph** is short and should not introduce any new information. Use it to **sum up** what you have written. You can also include a final thought, an evaluation, or a prediction about the future.

B ANALYZE THE MODEL Complete the tasks.

1. Highlight the thesis statement. Circle the claim the writer makes.

2. Highlight the topic sentences in paragraphs 2 and 3.

3. Circle a statistic in paragraph 2.

4. Circle an example in paragraph 3.

5. What does the author do in the conclusion? Choose the three best statements.

    a. Introduces new information

    b. Sums up the content of the essay

    c. Makes a comment on the content

    d. Makes a prediction about the future

    e. Rejects the claim made in the thesis statement

C APPLY For each topic sentence in the chart, write the letters of the matching supporting ideas and details. One idea is extra.

a. Harmful chemicals from farms are getting into our drinking water.

b. Global warming increases the risk of forest fires.

c. We are running out of landfills.

d. The supply of special metals used in electronics may run out in 20 years.

e. The average consumer throws away 70 pounds (32 kilograms) of clothing every year.

f. Less than 30 percent of our energy comes from renewable sources.

Topic sentences	Supporting ideas and details
1. In a linear economy, too much harmful waste is produced.	
2. Another problem with the linear economy is that resources are not used wisely.	

ReTuna, a shopping center in Eskilstuna, Sweden, sells only second-hand objects.

GRAMMAR The passive voice

The passive voice is made with a form of *be* + the past participle of the verb. The form of *be* indicates the time or aspect. The use of a modal + *be* shows possibility, necessity, etc.

Simple Present/Past: Too many resources **are/were wasted**.
Present/Past Continuous: Too many resources **are/were being wasted**.
Modal: Many of these resources **can/could be recycled.**

The passive voice is widely used in academic writing in the following ways.

1. To make generalizations, especially when the agent is unknown or unimportant.
   The agent is the person or thing that performs the action.

   Two-thirds of raw materials **are wasted** *(by people)*.

2. To improve how well the elements fit together (cohesion) by:
   ▸ keeping the same subject across clauses and sentences.

   Many metal components *are valuable, so* *they* **should be recycled**.
   subject   subject
   ▸ making the object of one clause or sentence the subject of the next one.

   The company raises and sells *fly larvae*. *These* **are then sold** *to fish farms.*
   object   subject

D GRAMMAR Rewrite these sentences in the passive. Don't include the agent.

1. Scientists are conducting studies to determine the impact of waste.

   _____

2. They will not release the results until next year.

   _____

3. Scientists say we must repeat these studies every few years.

   _____

4. We can't delay the move to the circular economy for much longer.

   _____

5. The research center is extending the deadline for applications.

   _____

6. We use too many raw materials in a linear economy.

   _____

7. Researchers will make recommendations to help reduce waste.

   _____

E GRAMMAR Rewrite the underlined clause in the passive. Don't include the agent.

1. The waste we send to landfills is increasing, <u>yet we could use it to make something useful.</u>

   _____

2. These products have parts that are easy to access <u>so that owners can repair or replace them.</u>

   _____

3. Tons of plastic ends up as waste, <u>although we could easily recycle it.</u>

   _____

4. Products are lasting longer <u>because businesses are designing them for a longer life.</u>

   _____

5. Smartphones contain valuable metals <u>which industries can extract to make new products.</u>

   _____

6. Consumers can buy higher-quality products <u>that they can repair, refurbish, or recycle.</u>

   _____

F GRAMMAR Complete the second sentence in the passive voice using your own ideas.

1. Many **raw materials** may soon run out. However, they _____

   _____

2. There are several ways to extend the life of **raw materials**. For example, they_____

   _____

3. **Food waste** is a big problem all over the world. However, it _____

   _____

4. Some companies are promoting usership of **products** instead of ownership. These products _____

   _____

G GRAMMAR Improve the cohesion of the paragraph. In your notebook, rewrite the sentences that include the word *people* using the passive.

Product packaging costs a lot, but people recycle very little of it. A new company in Santiago, Chile, Algramo, is hoping to change that, one bottle and bag at a time. When a bottle of soap is finished, people can return it to a vending machine at a supermarket. In fact, people can return the bottle over and over again. Each bottle has a special code, and each time people return it, the price of the soap is lower.

H EDIT Correct the six errors with the passive voice in the paragraph.

Most soaps and shampoos sell in plastic bottles. Most rice and beans sell in plastic bags. Unfortunately, most of this packaging is thrown away. Many consumers say they want manufacturers to reduce the amount of packaging that used in their products, especially plastic. Today, less plastic is being use in packaging than in the past, but more must be doing.

PLAN & WRITE

I BRAINSTORM Look back at the annotations you made on *Closing the Circle on Waste* and *The Rise of Usership*. Complete the chart. Add your own personal experiences or other details.

	Benefits of the linear economy for individuals	Benefits of the circular economy for individuals
Health and well-being		
Product quality, convenience, price		
Waste		
Jobs and wealth		
Personal experiences		

WRITING TIP

Be careful when you use personal experience as evidence in an essay. In general, it's not a good idea to use the first person (*I, me, my*). Instead, try to generalize your personal experience.

Too personal: *I threw away my old phone because it was too expensive to repair it.*

Better: *The high cost of repairs means many of us throw away our phones as soon as there is a problem.*

J OUTLINE Complete the outline for your essay. Choose the most important benefits for your body paragraphs.

Introductory paragraph   Hook: _____

_____

Background information: _____

_____

Thesis statement: _____

_____

First body paragraph   One benefit of the circular/linear economy for individuals is

_____

Supporting ideas/Details: _____

_____

_____

Second body paragraph   A linear/circular economy also benefits individuals because

_____

Supporting ideas/Details: _____

_____

_____

Concluding paragraph   In conclusion, _____

_____

K FIRST DRAFT Use your outline to write a first draft of your essay.

L REVISE Use this list as you write your second draft.

- ☐ Does your introductory paragraph catch the reader's attention?
- ☐ Does your thesis statement clearly express your claim about your topic?
- ☐ Do your body paragraphs provide evidence to support your thesis?
- ☐ Does your concluding paragraph contain no new information?

M EDIT Use this list as you write your final draft.

- ☐ Did you use the passive appropriately and in the correct form?
- ☐ Do your subjects and verbs agree?
- ☐ Do you use the correct verb forms?

N FINAL DRAFT Reread your final draft and correct any errors. Then submit it to your teacher.

REFLECT

A Check (✓) the Reflect activities you can do and the academic skills you can use.

☐ assess responsibility for reducing waste

☐ analyze your contribution to a circular economy

☐ evaluate ownership versus renting

☐ rank factors leading to change

☐ write an opinion essay about an economic model

☐ annotate text

☐ organize an essay

☐ the passive voice

☐ rank factors

B Write the vocabulary words from the unit in the correct column. Add any other words that you learned. Circle words you still need to practice.

NOUN	VERB	ADJECTIVE	ADVERB & OTHER

C Reflect on the ideas in the unit as you answer these questions.

1. Do you think you will make any changes in your own life because of what you have learned in the unit? Explain.

_____

_____

2. What is the most important thing you learned from this unit?

_____

_____

CHANGING HISTORY

The first photograph to show people, by Louis Daguerre, Paris, France, 1838

IN THIS UNIT

▶ Consider the history of food preservation

▶ Consider how preserved foods are part of your life

▶ Consider materials in the past and present

▶ Evaluate the role of plastic in history

▶ Write a problem-solution essay about an invention

SKILLS

READING
Make inferences

WRITING
Hedge your claims

GRAMMAR
Past with *used to* and *would*

CRITICAL THINKING
Understand hedging

CONNECT TO THE TOPIC

1. Look at the photo. How do you think the invention of photography changed history?

2. Think about something that you use every day. What do you know about that object's history?

WATCH

AN INSTANT SOLUTION

A display at the Cup Noodles Museum, Osaka, Japan

A PREVIEW Watch the video about the inventor of instant ramen, Momofuku Ando. Check (✓) the reason he wanted to invent instant ramen. ▶ 3.1

1. _____ To make a lot of money

2. _____ To feed hungry people

3. _____ To keep noodles fresh

4. _____ To become a celebrity

B Watch the excerpt from the video about the problem Ando faced. Complete the paragraph with the words. One word is extra. ▶ 3.2

bread	flour	noodles	rice	tasty	time

After World War II, there was a food shortage in Japan. So, the U.S. government sent a lot of ¹_____ and suggested that the Japanese use it to make ²_____. But Ando wanted to make ³_____ instead. He wanted them to be ⁴_____ and easy to make. He also wanted them to last a long ⁵_____ without a refrigerator. He tried many different methods to achieve these goals, but none of them worked.

C Watch the excerpt from the video. Complete the paragraph with the words. One word is extra. ▶ 3.3

fried	oil	packages	stay	success	wife

One day Ando was watching his ¹_____ cook dinner, and he got an idea. He ²_____ some noodles in hot ³_____. This removed all the water, so they would recook very quickly. His product was a big ⁴_____. He introduced his instant ramen in the 1950s and later, ramen in a cup in 1978. At that time, his company sold more than 40 billion ⁵_____ of noodles every year.

PREPARE TO READ

A VOCABULARY Read the sentences. Write the words in bold next to their definitions.

- You can **adapt** most recipes to feed more or fewer people.
- Millions of **bacteria** live on our skin and inside our bodies. Most are harmless.
- The food you eat begins to **break down** as soon as you put it in your mouth.
- Oxygen and water are both **critical** for human life.
- There is usually a **limitation** on the number of people allowed in the restaurant.
- Fruits and vegetables are more **nutritious** than cakes and candy.
- We can **preserve** fruits in cans and jars and eat them at a later time.
- Europeans began to cross the ocean and **settle** in North America in the mid-16th century.
- If you close a water bottle **tightly**, the water will not spill out.
- On weekends, the streets **transform** into a market for street vendors.

1. _____ (n pl) very small organisms that live everywhere and sometimes cause disease
2. _____ (v) to go live somewhere permanently
3. _____ (v) to prepare food so it does not go bad
4. _____ (n) something that controls or reduces activity
5. _____ (adv) firmly; in a way that is difficult to open again
6. _____ (adj) very important; necessary
7. _____ (v phr) to change chemically into smaller parts
8. _____ (v) to change completely
9. _____ (adj) containing substances that are necessary for growth and good health
10. _____ (v) to change something for different conditions or use

REFLECT   Consider the history of food preservation.

Before you read about how food is preserved, consider how preservation has changed over time and its impact on our lives. Discuss the questions in a small group.

1. In what ways is fresh food preserved today?
2. How do you think food was preserved in the past?
3. What impact do you think food preservation has had on our lives?

PRESERVED:
FROM FERMENTING
TO FREEZE-DRYING

Farmers hang persimmons to dry in Shandong Province, China.

A PREVIEW Read the first paragraph. How do you think the course of history might have been different without preserved food?

1   Picture this: You go to a supermarket and there's no frozen food, no cans of beans, or bottles of ketchup. It's hard to imagine a world without food that has been **preserved** in some way. Some historians believe that without preserved food, the course of history might have been very different.

Food to stay put

2   Fresh food doesn't stay fresh for very long. From the moment an animal is killed or a vegetable is picked, **bacteria** begins to **break** it **down**. Eventually, the food spoils[1] and, sometimes, becomes dangerous to eat. For early humans, this was a big problem because it meant that they had to eat animals soon after they were killed and eat fruits and vegetables soon after they were picked. This placed serious **limitations** on how they could live. They could not stay in one place; instead, they had to follow their food sources. In addition, they could not prepare for times when those food sources were not available. Preserving food solved many of these problems.

3   Preserving food requires controlling the conditions in which bacteria live. The bacteria will grow more slowly or die if their environment is not the right temperature, or if there is too much salt or not enough oxygen. Early humans succeeded in controlling these conditions without understanding how they worked. Arctic people took advantage of very low temperature by freezing fish and meat in order to preserve it. In hot, dry climates, people dried food, especially fruit and beans. In wetter climates, people often used salt or acids to preserve foods such as eggs, meat, and vegetables. One method, called fermentation[2], dates back more than 10,000 years and was used to make yogurt in the area that is now Iraq. Fermentation was probably discovered by accident when someone left some milk in a container and forgot about it. Returning days or weeks later, they found that the milk had **transformed** into yogurt.

4   Preserving food in these ways resulted in significant changes in how people lived. They had enough to eat even when there was no access to fresh food, and they were less likely to get sick from eating food that was full of dangerous bacteria. As a result, they were healthier and lived longer. Having a reliable food source also allowed them to **settle** in one place. Better health and settled communities resulted in larger populations, and eventually, these communities began to grow their own food, which allowed populations to increase even more.

Food on the go

5   Preserved food not only helped feed growing populations, it was also an important factor in worldwide trade, exploration, and war. By the 15th century, large ships allowed people to travel all over the world, but feeding the sailors was a challenge because the ships had no way to keep food fresh. A supply of preserved foods, including salted fish and meat, and dried beans, helped the sailors survive these long journeys. The food was probably not very tasty, but it was **nutritious** and kept the sailors alive, allowing global exploration to continue.

6   As global trade and exploration increased, the need to transport food easily and safely became **critical**. At the end of the 18th century, French armies were marching across three continents, but they didn't have enough to eat. In 1800, French leader Napoleon offered a reward for a new way to preserve food. A chef named Nicolas Appert found

[1]**spoil** (v) to lose freshness, especially when something is kept too long
[2]**fermentation** (n) a chemical process that changes the sugar in food

European Space Agency astronaut Luca Parmitano on the International Space Station

a way. He put food in glass jars, closed them **tightly**, and then heated them to a high temperature. The food inside the jars lasted for months. A few years later, a British inventor **adapted** Appert's method for cans and within a few decades, people could buy cans of soup, juice, vegetables, and meat.

7   Space exploration in the 20th century led to new forms of food preservation. It can cost $10,000 or more to send a pound of food into space, so reducing the weight of food is an important goal. Freeze-drying—a food preservation technique developed in the 1930s— helped solve this problem. Frozen food is placed in a machine, which extracts almost all of the water. A freeze-dried bowl of spaghetti, for example, can be reduced from a pound to an ounce (.45 kilograms to 28 grams). Astronauts simply add water and heat it.

8   While there are many more modern food preservation techniques, and new methods are always being developed, many people continue to enjoy food that has been preserved in traditional ways. This is true even when fresh food is available. These foods are often central to each culture's history and identity and are likely to remain favorites for generations to come.

B MAIN IDEAS Choose the three main ideas from the article.

a. Most people like traditional preserved foods.

b. Increased availability of food helped populations grow.

c. Food in space is not as heavy as the food we eat on Earth.

d. Preserved foods are just as healthy as fresh foods.

e. Preserved food allowed people to live in one place.

f. The availability of preserved food made longer journeys possible.

C DETAILS Write T for *True*, F for *False*, or *NG* for *Not Given* for each statement.

1. _____ Early humans needed to follow the animals that they hunted.

2. _____ Adding salt to food can preserve it.

3. _____ In China, eggs were preserved by placing them underground.

4. _____ A British inventor found a way to preserve food in jars.

5. _____ Many sailors died from eating poorly preserved food.

6. _____ Preserved food helped to feed armies.

D DETAILS Write the paragraph number (5–8) where each extra detail would fit best.

1. _____ There is a saying, "An army moves on its stomach."

2. _____ Some freeze-dried foods became popular back on Earth.

3. _____ Sailors often became very sick and weak on long ocean voyages.

4. _____ For example, dried salted fish remains popular in parts of Europe.

READING SKILL   Make inferences

Writers often imply ideas rather than directly stating them. In these cases, you will have to infer what the writer means. When you **make inferences**, you draw conclusions based on the information presented in the article as well as your background knowledge. For example:

The house burned down yesterday. The electrical system had not been updated since the 1940s.

These sentences present two facts but do not state the cause of the fire. You can infer that the cause was a problem in the electrical system because you know that electricity can cause fires. You also know that an old system is probably especially dangerous. This knowledge, together with the two facts, allows you to make the inference.

E APPLY Read the paragraph. Check (✓) the two inferences you can make. Use your knowledge from the article and the information in the paragraph.

   One of the earliest forms of food preservation is pickling, which can prevent food from spoiling for many years. People may have pickled foods as far back as 2000 BC. Most pickles are made by placing fruit, vegetables, meat, or eggs into either very salty water or an acid for several days. The most common acid is vinegar, which is a sour liquid made from fermented fruit. Pickled foods are popular all over the world. In the United States, the most popular pickled food is cucumbers—called pickles.

1. _____ American pickles mostly use vinegar.

2. _____ Pickled foods probably taste sour or salty.

3. _____ The liquids used in pickling likely slow the growth of bacteria.

4. _____ Pickling is the safest form of preservation.

F APPLY Read the paragraph in activity E again. Then check (✓) the four inferences you can make.

1. _____ We can't be sure when pickling first began.

2. _____ There may be other ways to pickle food than the two described in the paragraph.

3. _____ Vinegar is not the only acid used in pickling.

4. _____ Pickling is the most widely used form of food preservation in the United States.

5. _____ Cucumbers are not the only pickled food that is eaten in the United States.

G APPLY Read paragraph 6 of *Preserved: from Fermenting to Freeze-drying* again. Check (✓) the four inferences you can make. Explain how you made these inferences to a partner.

1. _____ Napoleon's army did not have access to much fresh food.

2. _____ Appert's method killed harmful bacteria in food.

3. _____ Appert received money for his invention.

4. _____ Appert understood that heat would kill the dangerous bacteria.

5. _____ Canned foods became more common than preserved food in jars.

REFLECT   Consider how preserved foods are part of your life.

Check (✓) the forms of preserved food that are common in your culture. Write down a food item preserved in this way. Then describe it to a partner. Say whether or not it is a food you enjoy, and why.

_____ dried food: _____   _____ pickled food: _____

_____ fermented food: _____   _____ salted food: _____

Pickled vegetables

PREPARE TO READ

A VOCABULARY Read the sentences. Choose the correct meaning for the words in bold.

1. Often, the main **drawback** of a plan is that it is too expensive.

   a. idea   b. disadvantage   c. cost

2. Many people think that real plants are more attractive than **fake** ones.

   a. flowering   b. wild   c. not real

3. Some tree branches don't break even in strong wind because they are **flexible**.

   a. able to bend   b. heavy   c. growing

4. Items made of glass are usually **fragile**, so you need to handle them carefully.

   a. difficult to use   b. expensive   c. easily broken

5. Smartphones should make our lives easier, but **ironically**, they often do the opposite.

   a. in an unexpected way   b. obviously   c. in a way that is hard to understand

6. **Luxury** items should be taxed more than everyday items like food and clothes.

   a. popular   b. very expensive but not necessary   c. imported from other countries

7. It is difficult to grow crops in areas where water is **scarce**.

   a. far away   b. hard to find   c. on the ground

8. New shoes are often **stiff** and uncomfortable.

   a. attractive   b. difficult to find   c. hard to bend

9. Text messaging **took off** in the late 1990s and is still popular today.

   a. suddenly became successful   b. was a surprise   c. made a profit

10. A long electrical **wire** connects a table lamp to an outlet in a wall.

    a. thin piece of metal   b. signal   c. piece of cloth

REFLECT Consider materials in the past and present.

You are going to read about the history of plastic. Before you read, answer the questions. Then discuss your ideas with a partner.

1. What objects do you own that are made of plastic? Write three objects for each category.

   In your bag: _____

   In your bathroom: _____

   In your refrigerator: _____

2. What material (wood, paper, metal, etc.) do you think these objects were made of before plastic was invented?

THE PLASTIC **REVOLUTION**

🎧 3.2

1 Many of the ordinary things that we use every day, from combs to toothbrushes, were once **luxury** items. They were available only to the rich. They were made from natural raw materials, such as silver and ivory[1], which were **scarce** and expensive. Plastic changed all that. It freed us from natural materials. There was an almost unlimited supply of plastic, and it could be made with specific characteristics—hard or soft, **stiff** or **flexible**, clear or colored. And it was inexpensive, which allowed hundreds of thousands of people to become consumers for the first time. A plastic comb or toothbrush came at a price almost anyone could pay. In many ways, plastic has been a great equalizer[2] in society.

2 There is a common expression: "Necessity is the mother of invention," and the first plastic was invented to answer a specific but surprising need— for more billiard balls. In the 19th century, billiard balls were made from ivory, but the ivory trade was destroying the elephant population. Billiards[3] was a game for the rich, and many of these people were worried that the supply of balls would run out. So, a $10,000 reward was offered to anyone who could find something to replace the ivory in billiard balls. In 1869, the inventor John Wesley Hyatt came up with a material he called "celluloid." Unfortunately for him, it did not work very well for billiard balls, but it worked very well in the new field of photography, where it was cut into thin slices to make film. Before celluloid film, photographers had used glass plates, which were heavy, expensive, and **fragile**. In comparison, celluloid was cheap and light.

3 Electricity presented another problem that was solved by plastic. In the early 20th century, electricity was becoming an important source of power, but it caused frequent fires. Electrical **wires** were covered in order to prevent these fires. However, the material used at the time came from an insect found only in India and Thailand, which was expensive. In 1907 Leo Baekeland, a chemist, came up with a better solution. He created a new material from coal waste, which he called Bakelite. It didn't melt, burn, rust[4], or break down, and it could be made into different

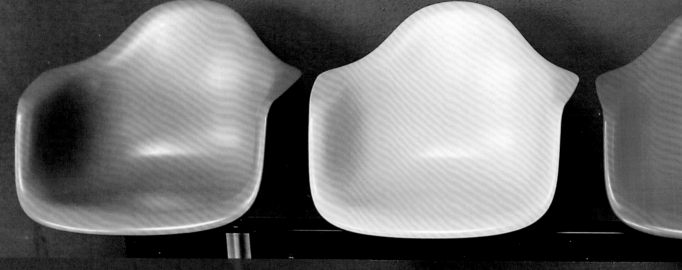

A PREDICT Read the title and the first paragraph. What do you think the article is mostly about?

a. How plastics have changed in the last century

b. The ways plastic has solved some problems

c. The dangers of plastic to human health

shapes, including the shape of an electrical wire. This development significantly increased the safety of using electricity, and it was an important factor in the success of 20th-century electrification. Within a few years, scientists began inventing all kinds of similar materials. First called "plastics" in 1925, these materials reduced the need for raw materials such as wood, rubber, and metal, and they were light, flexible, strong, waterproof, fireproof, but best of all, inexpensive.

4   In the 1950s, plastic production **took off**. Hundreds of products became available to a whole new group of consumers, not just the rich. Plastic had reached a turning point. It was no longer used simply to replace natural raw materials. Designers began to explore this strong but flexible material in new and creative ways. They made plastic exciting, fashionable, and accessible to a generation of young consumers. Furniture designers Charles and Ray Eames, for example, wanted to design chairs that were "the best for the most for the least." They chose plastic as their material and produced a prize-winning design that was attractive, yet inexpensive. The design remains popular today.

5   After a time, however, plastic began to lose its positive image. The public began to see plastic products as **fake** and low-quality. In addition,

starting in the 1960s, public awareness of plastic waste began to increase. **Ironically**, one of plastic's greatest advantages—it doesn't rust or break down like metal or wood—became its greatest **drawback**. Since 1955, we have produced about 8 billion tons of plastic waste, and almost all of it is still here. In addition, most plastic is made from fossil fuels.

6   Today, scientists are working on both sides of the plastic problem. Some are researching chemicals that can break down plastics, as well as bacteria that will eat it. Other scientists are hoping to replace fossil fuels as the raw material for making plastic. Bioplastics are made from algae[5] and, often, corn or sugar cane. Compared to plastics made from fossil fuels, these bioplastics break down quickly. Since its invention, plastic has solved many problems, but it has also created new ones. Fortunately, these new research projects may lead to solutions.

---

[1]**ivory** (n) the material in an elephant's tusk

[2]**equalizer** (n) something that makes things or people equal

[3]**billiards** (n) a game in which players use a stick to hit balls into holes along the edges of a table

[4]**rust** (v) to become covered in a red substance that comes from mixing iron, air, and water

[5]**algae** (n pl) small, simple plants that live in bodies of water

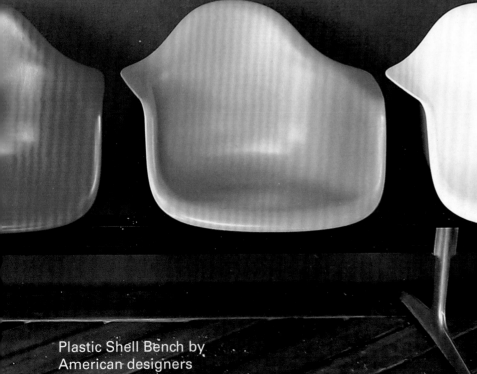

Plastic Shell Bench by American designers Charles and Ray Eames

B MAIN IDEAS Choose the four main ideas of the article.

a. Plastic is inexpensive and has many positive characteristics.

b. Bioplastics are better for the environment.

c. Plastic was first used to replace expensive raw materials.

d. Plastic made more products available to a larger group of consumers.

e. The history of plastics also has a negative side.

f. The first plastic was quite expensive but gradually decreased in price.

C MAIN IDEAS Choose the best alternative title for the article. Explain your choice to a partner.

a. Where Would We Be Without Plastics?

b. Plastics: A Success Story

c. The Rise and Fall of Plastics

D DETAILS Complete the summary. Use one word from the article for each answer.

Plastic has several benefits. It replaced many scarce and expensive

1_____ materials. It is light, inexpensive, and can be made

into many different 2_____. Plastic made products accessible

to a much larger group of 3_____. However, plastic's biggest

4_____ is that it breaks down very, very slowly. Plastic,

therefore, creates a great deal of 5_____. Today, scientists are

researching new plastics that break down more 6_____.

E Check (✓) four inferences that you can make based on information in the article and your own knowledge.

1. _____ Plastic is not considered a natural material. (paragraph 1)

2. _____ Hyatt did not get the $10,000 reward. (paragraph 2)

3. _____ Bakelite was a good replacement for ivory. (paragraph 3)

4. _____ Bakelite was cheaper than the material made from insects. (paragraph 3)

5. _____ Early plastic products were very popular. (paragraph 4)

6. _____ Plastic chairs were more popular than wooden or metal chairs. (paragraph 4)

7. _____ The production of plastic adds to global warming. (paragraphs 5 and 6)

Bakelite and early plastic objects at the Bakelite Museum, Minehead, UK

Evaluate the role of plastic in history.

Complete the chart with all the pros and cons of plastic that you can think of. Then use your lists to discuss this question in a small group: Do you think the invention of plastic has been a good or a bad thing?

Plastic	
Pros	Cons

WRITE

Typists take part in a speed competition while wearing blindfolds in Paris, France, 1939.

UNIT TASK   Write a problem-solution essay about an invention.

You are going to write an essay in response to the question, "Think of an object. What problems did the invention of this object solve?" Use the ideas, vocabulary, and skills from the unit.

A MODEL Read the model essay. Do you agree with the writer's claim that typewriters revolutionized businesses? Discuss your ideas with a partner.

The Typewriter: Business Problems Solved

1   Do you write your essays on a laptop or tablet? Most students probably do. But ask your grandparents what they used to use and they are likely to say, "a typewriter." In fact, at one time, students leaving home to go to college would receive a typewriter as a gift, a sign that they had become adults. Typewriters now seem old-fashioned, but in the 19th century they helped change the world. The invention of the typewriter solved a number of problems, revolutionizing many 19th-century businesses.

2   Before typewriters, keeping business records was a manual process. In the 19th century, businesses were expanding all over the world. All these new offices and factories had to keep records. This paperwork took a long time because business, legal, and even medical records

used to be written by hand. Thousands of workers just wrote and copied these records. The fastest workers could write about 30 words per minute, but most were much slower because they had to be careful to write clearly and not to make any mistakes.

3 Handwriting can be difficult to read, which sometimes led to errors. For example, the wrong quantities of a product were sometimes shipped to the wrong place at the wrong time. To avoid errors, businesses would sometimes take really important documents to a professional printer, but this was expensive.

4 The typewriter addressed these problems. Typewritten documents were easy to read because all typewriters used similar type, so the documents looked almost the same. While early models would stop working when the keys were hit too fast, a new design overcame that issue. This design placed the most common letters far apart on the keyboard. With this keyboard, many typists could easily reach a speed of about 50–60 words per minute. This was far faster than writing by hand. Importantly for businesses, buying a typewriter was cheaper than using a professional printing press.

5 With the invention of the typewriter, many businesses became more efficient and saved money. The typewriter was a good invention, but there were problems that typewriters could not solve, such as correcting, copying, and storing documents. All those problems had to wait for the invention of the personal computer at the end of the 20th century.

B **ANALYZE THE MODEL** Complete the tasks.

1. Underline the background information that the writer provides in the introductory paragraph.
2. Highlight the claim the writer makes in the thesis statement.
3. Underline the topic sentence in each body paragraph. Then check (✓) whether the paragraph is mainly about a problem or solution.

   a. Paragraph 2   _____ **Problem**   _____ **Solution**
   b. Paragraph 3   _____ **Problem**   _____ **Solution**
   c. Paragraph 4   _____ **Problem**   _____ **Solution**

4. What information does the concluding paragraph include? Choose the two best answers.

   a. A summary of how typewriters solved business problems
   b. A prediction about the future of typewriters
   c. An evaluation of the typewriter
   d. Other problems the typewriter solved

WRITING SKILL Hedge your claims

It is important not to overgeneralize or to make your claims too strong in your writing. You can soften your claims, or **hedge**, in several ways.

1. Express possibility with adverbs, adjectives, and modals.
    Strong claim: *These foods will remain favorites.*
    Softer claims: *These foods will **probably** remain favorites.*
                        *These foods are **likely** to remain favorites.*
                        *These foods **may** remain favorites.*

2. Use quantifiers and frequency modifiers.
    Overgeneralization: *All cultures have found ways to preserve food.*
    Softer claim: ***Most** cultures have found ways to preserve food.*

    Overgeneralization: *Electricity causes fires.*
    Softer claim: *Electricity **sometimes** causes fires.*

3. Qualify cause-and-effect statements.
    Strong claim: *Preserved food increased global trade.*
    Softer claims: *Preserved foods **were one factor** in growing global trade.*
                        *Preserved foods **helped** increase global trade.*

C APPLY Review the introductory paragraph in the model. Highlight four words that hedge the claims in it.

D APPLY Complete the sentences. Use softer claims.

1. Preserving food _____ solve the problems of hunger.

2. _____ early humans _____ died from eating food that was full of dangerous bacteria.

3. The first fermentation _____ happened by accident.

4. Drying is _____ the best method for preserving foods.

5. In the past, _____ homes had cellars under the house to store vegetables for the winter.

E APPLY Rewrite the following sentences. Use softer claims.

1. Rich people played billiards.

    _____

2. The glass plates used by photographers broke.

    _____

3. The manufacturing of plastic causes global warming.

    _____

4. Bioplastics are better for the environment.

    _____

Before film, photographers used to use glass plates.

F NOTICE THE GRAMMAR Look back at the model essay. Underline the past habits expressed with *used to* or *would*. Then choose the sentence that best describes the examples. Explain your choice to a partner.

a. Actions that happened once in the past and then stopped

b. Actions that happened regularly in the past but don't anymore

c. Actions that were in progress for a period of time in the past

GRAMMAR   Past with *used to* and *would*

Used to and ***would*** describe past habits that no longer occur. *Used to* can describe an action or state that happened repeatedly or continued for a long time in the past. *Would* only describes actions or states that happened repeatedly, not things that continued for a long time. *Used to* and *would* are followed by the base form of the verb.

> In the 18th century, people **used to/would write** their documents by hand.
>
> He **used to live** in Belgium. (NOT: ~~He would live in Belgium.~~)
>
> I **used to love** writing letters. (NOT: ~~I would love writing letters.~~)

It is common to use *used to, would,* and simple past together. In longer passages, we often begin with *used to* and continue with *would* or the simple past.

> In the 18th century, people **used to write** all their documents by hand. They **would** carefully **write** each word with pen and ink, and then they **let** the ink dry.

G GRAMMAR Complete the sentences with *used to* or *used to/would*. (Three sentences can only use *used to*.)

1. In the 1940s, people _____ listen to the news on the radio every night.

2. When he was a child, my father _____ take the bus to school.

3. When we were kids, we _____ play basketball in the evenings.

4. As a teenager, she _____ be much thinner.

5. As children, they _____ go to the library every week.

6. When he was a student, he _____ live in Japan.

7. During the holidays, my house _____ always smell like apple pie.

8. When I was growing up, I _____ have a pet lizard.

H PERSONALIZE How is your life different now from the past? Complete the sentences with *used to* and your own ideas.

1. When I was a child, my family _____.

2. My first teacher _____.

3. When I was younger, my favorite food _____.

4. This school _____.

5. People in my hometown _____.

6. Most of my friends _____.

I EDIT Find and correct five errors in the use of *used to* and *would* in the paragraph.

The First Plastic: Bakelite

Everything from watches to radios would be made of Bakelite. But what is Bakelite, and where does it come from? Bakelite was the very first plastic, and it was invented by Leo Baekeland, who was born in Belgium in 1863. As a boy, he would love chemistry and physics. He used study for hours every day and do science experiments at home. At 24, he was already teaching at a university. That's also when he began his career as an inventor. Baekeland wanted to invent something to cover electric wires safely. Without some sort of covering, electrical wiring would to often cause fires. Every day, he use to go into his basement and try something new. It took him almost 10 years, but he finally came up with a substance that worked. He called it Bakelite.

PLAN & WRITE

J BRAINSTORM Follow the steps.

1. What would your life be like without these inventions? Discuss your ideas in a small group. Then think of two other objects you might want to write about.

ballpoint pen	contact lenses	laptop	camera
bicycle	earbuds	smartphone	refrigerator

Two other objects: _____   _____

2. Choose one of the inventions and complete the chart. Research the history of this invention or ask a person familiar with what was used before for ideas.

What did people do or use before the object was invented?	
What problems did people have before the object was invented? List two or three.	
How did the invention solve these problems? Why was it a good solution?	
How would you evaluate the success of the invention? Did it change how people live and work?	

WRITING TIP

You can use the following phrases to talk about problems and solutions.

Problems	**Solutions**
had drawbacks/disadvantages	*solved the problem*
caused issues/problems	*overcame the objections/issues*
was difficult to (do something)	*was a good solution*
was a challenge	

*The typewriter **had** two **drawbacks**. . . . The invention of the personal computer **solved these problems**.*

K OUTLINE Complete the outline using the ideas you developed in activity J.

Introductory paragraph Hook: _____

Background information: _____

Thesis statement: _____

First body paragraph Problem 1: _____

_____

Supporting ideas/Details: _____

_____

Second body paragraph Problem 2: _____

_____

Supporting ideas/Details: _____

_____

Third body paragraph Solution: _____

_____

Supporting ideas/Details: _____

_____

Concluding paragraph Summary: _____

Evaluation: _____

L FIRST DRAFT Use your outline to write a first draft of your essay.

M REVISE Use this list as you write your second draft.

☐ Does your introduction have a hook that will catch the reader's attention?

☐ Does your thesis statement clearly express your claim about the invention?

☐ Do your body paragraphs adequately describe the problems?

☐ Do your body paragraphs describe how your object solved the problems?

☐ Does your conclusion evaluate the impact of the object?

N EDIT Use this list as you write your final draft.

☐ Did you use the past with *used to* and *would* correctly?

☐ Did you hedge your claims appropriately?

☐ Did you use the correct verb forms?

☐ Do your subjects and verbs agree?

☐ Did you use the vocabulary of problems and solutions (see the Writing Tip)?

O FINAL DRAFT Reread your essay and correct any errors. Then submit it to your teacher.

REFLECT

A Check (✓) the Reflect activities you can do and the academic skills you can use.

- ☐ consider the history of food preservation
- ☐ consider how preserved foods are part of your life
- ☐ consider materials in the past and present
- ☐ evaluate the role of plastic in history
- ☐ write a problem-solution essay about an invention

- ☐ make inferences
- ☐ hedge your claims
- ☐ past with *used to* and *would*
- ☐ understand hedging

B Write the vocabulary words from the unit in the correct column. Add any other words that you learned. Circle words you still need to practice.

NOUN	VERB	ADJECTIVE	ADVERB & OTHER

C Reflect on the ideas in the unit as you answer these questions.

1. What did you learn that surprised you?

_____

_____

2. Are you now more curious about the history of the things you use every day? What other objects would you like to know more about?

_____

_____

3. What is the most important thing you learned from this unit?

_____

_____

LEADING BUSINESSES

Mark Kamau, an entrepreneur in Nairobi, Kenya, holds a prototype for a mobile weather station.

CONNECT TO THE TOPIC

1. Look at the photo and read the caption. How could his invention be useful?

2. Do you know of any famous entrepreneurs? What are they famous for?

69

CHANGING THE **JEWELRY BUSINESS**

Jewelry making,
Bangkok, Thailand

A You are going to watch a video about Proud Limpongpan, an entrepreneur who makes jewelry. Watch the video. Complete the sentence about Limpongpan's main goal for her business. ▶ 4.1

She wants to make her jewelry business more _____.

B Watch the video again. Choose the correct answers. ▶ 4.1

1. What is the problem with most jewelry-making businesses?

   a. They pollute the air.

   b. The jewelry can harm the skin of people who wear it.

   c. They produce toxic chemicals.

2. What do most jewelry businesses do about this problem?

   a. They charge more money to produce sustainable jewelry.

   b. They put the harmful chemicals into the environment.

   c. They say that there is no problem.

3. What will Ennovie do to solve this problem?

   a. It will store harmful substances in a safe place.

   b. It will be more honest with its customers.

   c. It will change the chemicals so they aren't harmful.

C Does Ennovie's business plan make you more or less likely to buy jewelry from them? Discuss your answer with a partner.

PREPARE TO READ

A VOCABULARY Read the sentences. Write the words in bold next to their definitions.

▶ I think your project is too **ambitious**. There is a lot to finish before the deadline.

▶ **Assertive** people usually make good salespeople because they aren't afraid to speak up.

▶ A good boss gives his or her employees a lot of **credit** for a successful year.

▶ If you are **determined**, you will succeed in spite of any problems.

▶ Digital innovation can **disrupt** traditional businesses. For example, more people now use ride-hailing companies like Uber than traditional taxis.

▶ Car owners are often required to buy **insurance** in case of a car accident.

▶ It is useful to have a **network** of colleagues who can give you career advice.

▶ Most salespeople **pursue** a goal of increasing their sales every year.

▶ Before its release in 2008, Apple did a **remarkable** job of keeping the iPhone a secret.

▶ Some people think that parking a car in a parking garage is more **secure** than parking on the street.

1. _____ (v) to try hard to achieve something
2. _____ (adj) confident and direct
3. _____ (n) praise and approval
4. _____ (adj) unusually good; special
5. _____ (v) to change the traditional way that something works
6. _____ (adj) requiring a great deal of time, effort, and skill to achieve
7. _____ (adj) wanting something a lot and not letting anything stop you
8. _____ (n) protection against a future problem
9. _____ (adj) safe; without risk
10. _____ (n) a group of people or organizations that are connected

B PERSONALIZE Discuss these questions with a partner.

1. Can you describe a time when you were **determined** to do something, but other people told you not to do it?

2. Do you think it is good to be **assertive** when you are in a group? Or is it better to keep quiet even if you don't agree, so that everyone remains friendly? Explain.

REFLECT Compare types of businesses.

You are going to read a profile of an entrepreneur from Colombia. How do you think that businesses started by entrepreneurs are different from other businesses? Discuss the following areas in a small group.

| kind of business (e.g., finance, manufacturing) | size | customer profile |
| type/number of employees | location | purpose |

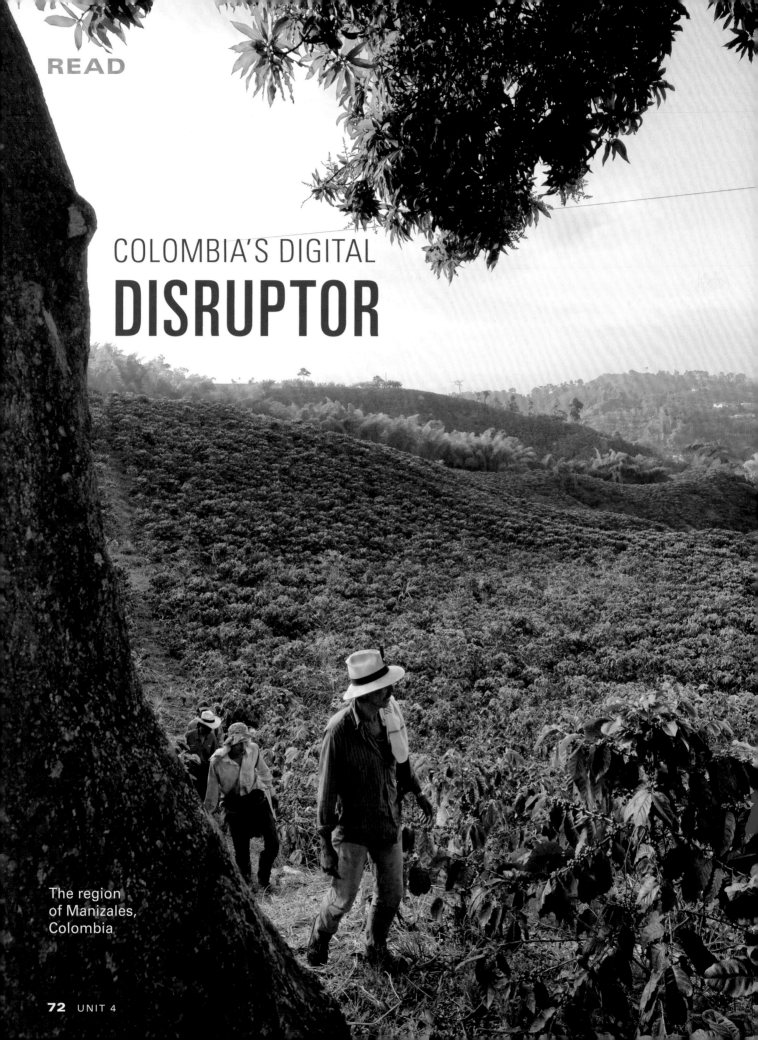

COLOMBIA'S DIGITAL
DISRUPTOR

The region
of Manizales,
Colombia

A PREDICT Read the introduction and the questions in the profile. What do you think the answers to the questions will be? Then read and compare your answers.

🎧 4.1

The business world loves entrepreneurs—think of Steve Jobs, Elon Musk, and Carlos Slim. With a **remarkable** *ability to do things differently, today's entrepreneurs are* **disrupting** *markets from finance to technology. One example is Andrés Gutiérrez, a young entrepreneur from Colombia.*

What does Andrés Gutiérrez do?

1   Gutiérrez is a Colombian businessman who has already founded one successful company. He is now working on a second company, an **ambitious** project that Gutiérrez hopes will provide mobile financial services to 400 million people across Latin America who do not have bank accounts.

What is his background? Did he always want to be an entrepreneur?

2   Not at all. He says as a child, he was very shy and his family had to push him to be more **assertive**. His grandmother, who owned an avocado[1] farm, made him go around the neighborhood selling avocados in an effort to build his self-confidence. He went on to get a business degree in Bogotá and then got a job in a company in the United States that manufactures cans, so he was on a pretty traditional business career path.

So, what changed? Why did he decide to become an entrepreneur?

3   In the United States, he watched as new businesses, particularly online businesses and mobile apps, were beginning to disrupt markets such as air travel and taxis. He asked friends at home if this was happening in Colombia. In Mexico, Argentina, and Brazil, the trend was starting, but not in Colombia, they told him, though smartphones were growing in popularity. Realizing that this was an opportunity, he decided to leave his **secure** job in the United States and start a ride-hailing service in Colombia, which uses an app, much like Uber. "My father was scared," says Gutiérrez. "He was terrified that I was leaving this stable job," but Gutiérrez was **determined** to **pursue** his idea. He was sure it was the right time.

4   In 2012, he found a business partner with the right technical skills and together they founded Tappsi, a business that quite quickly became successful, serving 1.6 million riders a month. Less than a year later, someone offered to buy the company for a million dollars, but they turned the offer down. "I remember my father's face at dinner when I told him I didn't accept it," Gutiérrez recalls. His father told him, "You have no idea what you just did, Andrés. You have no idea how long it takes to build 1 million dollars!" But Gutiérrez was firm, eventually selling the company for much, much more.

---

[1]**avocado** (n) a green, pear-shaped tropical fruit

It's a big jump from a ride-hailing company to mobile finance. How did that happen?

5 It actually happened quite naturally, Gutiérrez recalls. While he was working on Tappsi, he realized one of the biggest problems in his business occurred at the point of payment. Most riders wanted to pay by credit card or phone, but the drivers accepted only cash. Gutiérrez thought, "This is crazy! It's 2018!" and then he discovered that most of his drivers did not have bank accounts. That is when the idea hit him. And it wasn't just the Tappsi drivers. A huge number of people in Colombia and across Latin America work in the informal economy—the cash-based economy that operates outside of the banking and government systems. The consequences for these people are enormous.

6 In a 2019 interview, Gutiérrez gave the example of a coffee farmer who had to walk five miles (8.5 kilometers) to the nearest town to pay his electricity bill or to send money to pay for his son's school. Whenever he sent or received money in this way, he had to pay a 5 percent fee. Even worse, because all his farm business was done in cash, he had no records of his income, and without records, he could not get a loan or **insurance**. This farmer's experience was very common. In fact, Gutiérrez estimates that there are about 400 million people like him in Latin America. So, he decided to start a new business, Tpaga, a mobile wallet that drivers, farmers, and anyone else can use to send and receive money digitally. Soon, he hopes to add other financial services, such as loans and insurance, all available on a smartphone.

What lessons has he learned, and what advice would he give to his "younger self"?

7 Gutiérrez gives a lot of **credit** to the people who have worked with him, stressing the importance of having a great team, where each team member has different knowledge and skills. He offers his employees equity[2] in the company, which means that the harder they work, the more money they can make. He believes that having a **network** of people who can support you and give you advice is also essential. If he could start all over again, with Tappsi, he says his advice would be to set more ambitious goals from the beginning. Finally, you need to love your job. If you don't love it, stop doing it.

---

[2]**equity** (n) a share in the ownership of a company

Tappsi disrupted the taxi industry in Colombia.

B MAIN IDEAS Choose the correct answers.

1. Which factor has been the most important in Gutiérrez's business success?

    a. He had a good background in business and technology.

    b. He recognized a good opportunity and pursued it.

    c. He has good leadership skills, and people want to work with him.

    d. He has the right kind of personality to be an entrepreneur: He is assertive and energetic.

2. What do Gutiérrez's two businesses have in common?

    a. They provide a service that was not available before.

    b. They save users money.

    c. They became very popular immediately.

    d. They required a large investment to get started.

C DETAILS Complete the summary. Use one word from the profile for each answer.

While Gutiérrez was working in the United States, he saw how technology was changing

traditional ¹_____, such as the airline industry. When his friends told him that this

had not yet happened yet in Colombia, he realized that he had a(n) ²_____ to get

ahead of the competition. He decided to start a business that would disrupt the

³_____ market. In less than a year, the business had become a great success.

Someone ⁴_____ Gutiérrez a million dollars for the company, but he said no.

Before long, he was ready for his next challenge, a mobile ⁵_____ that provides

financial services for people who do not have a bank ⁶_____.

D DETAILS Read each statement. Write T for *True*, F for *False*, or NG for *Not Given* based on the information in the profile.

1. _____ Gutiérrez got a business degree because he wanted to be an entrepreneur.

2. _____ Gutiérrez decided not to continue on a traditional career path.

3. _____ Most Tappsi riders did not have bank accounts.

4. _____ Many people in Colombia work outside of the formal economy.

5. _____ People without bank accounts have trouble getting financial services.

6. _____ People who use cell phones pay fees for financial services.

7. _____ Tpaga is used by 400 million people in Latin America.

8. _____ Tpaga users can now buy insurance through the app.

9. _____ Tpaga is more profitable than Tappsi.

10. _____ Gutiérrez acknowledges the contributions of people on his team.

READING SKILL Find evidence

In school and college, you often need to **find evidence** to support an argument you want to make in a presentation, essay, or report. For example, you may need to look for evidence to support a claim you are making in your thesis statement. Follow these steps when you need to find evidence in a text.

1. Read the article all the way through so that you have a good general understanding of it.
2. Read the article for a second time, thinking about your writing task (e.g., a question you want to answer or a claim you want to support).
3. Annotate parts of the article that will help with your writing task.

E APPLY Which of these claims are supported by evidence in the profile? Check (✓) if there is evidence in support of the claim. Write *x* if there is evidence against the claim.

1. _____ Entrepreneurs come from the United States. (paragraph 1)

2. _____ They have a business education. (paragraph 2)

3. _____ They are prepared to take risks. (paragraph 3)

4. _____ They start businesses that disrupt markets. (paragraph 3)

5. _____ They fail the first time they start a business. (paragraph 4)

6. _____ They start more than one business. (paragraph 6)

F APPLY Review the claims in activity E. Highlight the evidence in the profile in support of or against each claim. There may be more than one piece of evidence. Compare your answers with a partner.

REFLECT Interpret a pie chart about businesses.

Look at the pie chart and answer the questions. Discuss your ideas with a partner.

1. What are the two most common reasons entrepreneurs start a business?

2. Can you think of any other reasons why an entrepreneur would start a business?

3. How would you describe Gutiérrez's main reason(s) for becoming an entrepreneur?

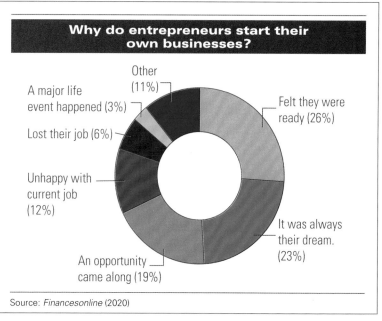

Why do entrepreneurs start their own businesses?

- Other (11%)
- A major life event happened (3%)
- Lost their job (6%)
- Unhappy with current job (12%)
- An opportunity came along (19%)
- Felt they were ready (26%)
- It was always their dream. (23%)

Source: *Financesonline* (2020)

PREPARE TO READ

A VOCABULARY Read the sentences. Discuss the meaning of the words in bold with a partner. Then write the words next to their definitions.

▸ This jewelry might **appeal to** you because it is made in a sustainable way.

▸ Most university students will begin to **contemplate** their futures as they near graduation.

▸ We are hoping that the **current** situation will not last very long.

▸ If you miss too many classes, there will be a **gap** in your knowledge.

▸ In some factories, workers wear gloves to protect their hands from **harmful** chemicals.

▸ One wealthy **investor** gave 10 million dollars to help start the company.

▸ The company was unable to deliver the product on time because of a major **setback**.

▸ Factories need to have a dependable **supply** of raw materials.

▸ Family and friends are often very **supportive** when you lose your job.

▸ The rough **texture** of a wool scarf can scratch your skin.

1. _____ (n) something missing
2. _____ (n) something that stops or slows a process
3. _____ (adj) causing hurt or damage
4. _____ (v phr) to attract; to please
5. _____ (n) the way something feels when you touch it
6. _____ (v) to think about carefully
7. _____ (adj) happening now
8. _____ (n) amount available
9. _____ (n) a person who puts money into a company
10. _____ (adj) helpful and encouraging

REFLECT Relate data to a business opportunity.

You are going to read about an entrepreneur trying to solve a problem with a food source. Study the graph and answer the questions. Discuss your ideas with a partner.

1. What does the graph show about the future of seafood? Why is this a problem?

2. What do you think is the reason for this trend?

3. How could businesses help solve this problem?

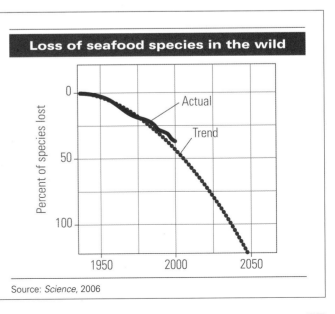

Loss of seafood species in the wild

Source: *Science*, 2006

READ

THE
SHRIMP MAKERS

🎧 4.2

A PREDICT Read the title and look at Figure 1. What do you think the article is mostly about?

a. New methods of fishing

b. How to protect seafood from harmful chemicals

c. Growing seafood in a laboratory

1   Sandhya Sriram has loved science ever since she was a child growing up in India and the Middle East. At first, she thought she might become a doctor, but then she decided to become a scientist, where she hoped to make medical discoveries that would improve people's lives. She worked with human stem cells[1], searching for ways to stop heart disease and cancer, but after several years working in the field, she started to become impatient. The process of finding new drugs and other therapies had too many **setbacks** and seemed to take forever, so she began to look for other ways to use her creative energy. First, she started a company focused on science education. That's when she first thought of herself as an entrepreneur. She continued to wonder: how could she keep doing the science that she loved, but use her knowledge to create something new? How could she do something that would make the world a better place and make money at the same time?

2   Sriram took business courses while she considered the best place to start. She had a **supportive** mentor[2], who told her that although many people have excellent

Sandhya Sriram and her partner, Ka Yi Ling, Singapore

Shiok **Meats**

ideas, successful entrepreneurs are able to match those ideas to a **gap** in the market—to something that is missing but the public will want. They recognize an opportunity, and they pursue it. Sriram considered a number of different opportunities, but one in particular **appealed to** her—how to feed the world's growing population.

3   It is estimated that the global population will reach 9.8 billion by 2050, and more and more of that population is eating seafood. That's a problem because researchers warn that **current** levels of fishing are not sustainable and that the global **supply** of seafood may run out by then. In addition, as a result of pollution, wild seafood often contains plastic and **harmful** chemicals. In response to these problems, seafood from farms has begun to replace wild seafood in the market, yet these farms have their own problems. In many of them, the animals grow in dirty conditions, and they are given drugs in order to keep them healthy.

4   To solve this problem, some entrepreneurs are disrupting the market with plant-based "meat." This idea has been particularly popular with vegetarians like Sriram, who do not want animals to be killed for their food. Unfortunately, most plant-based meats do not have the same taste or **texture** as real meat, nor do they provide the same nutrition. Sriram also knew there were a lot of people who did not want to give up meat but still wanted to help the planet and eat healthy food. She thought she had a better idea that would solve all of these problems for the seafood market—real seafood grown in a laboratory from the stem cells of real animals. She had worked with stem cells for years when she was a scientist, so she understood the process. "Why not do the same thing with animal stem cells?" she asked herself. At the time, a few companies had started using this process to create "clean meat," but no one else was working on "clean seafood" (see Figure 1). She realized that she had found her gap in the market. Based in Singapore, Sriram decided to focus first on growing shrimp, which is a $25 billion market in Asia.

[1] **stem cell** (n) a cell from an early stage of development that can grow into any kind of cell (e.g., muscle, skin)

[2] **mentor** (n) a person who gives advice and support to someone with less experience

How to create "clean" shrimp

1. Collect stem cells from shrimp.

2. Grow the stem cells with a special mix of nutrients.

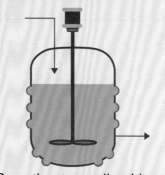

3. Form the mix into food items, like dumplings.

Figure 1   Source: Shiok Meats

5   With another scientist, Ka Yi Ling, and the support of **investors** and the Singapore government, she founded a company, Shiok Meats, in 2018. Their goal was to grow "clean" shrimp from shrimp stem cells in a laboratory. The word *shiok* is local slang[3] that means delicious or fantastic. The company, the first "clean" seafood company in the world, spent two years developing its first product, as well as raising almost $8 million from investors. In 2020, Shiok Meats presented shrimp grown in their labs to the public for the first time. A local chef, who tasted the shrimp dumplings[4], said she could not tell that they were not made with shrimp from the ocean. It looked, smelled, and tasted like shrimp. Even Sriram tried them since Shiok shrimp does not require killing any animals.

6   Sriram looks back on her achievement but knows that there is a lot more to do. When people ask her the secret to her success, she says that you must believe in what you are doing and you must love doing it. "Be fearless and just do it," she says. "If you're just sitting there and **contemplating**, things will never move forward . . . if you have an idea that you can't get out of your head, just go for it!"

[3]**slang** (n) informal language
[4]**dumpling** (n) chopped meat, seafood, or vegetables wrapped in dough

B MAIN IDEAS Write the paragraph number (1–6) next to its main idea. One idea is extra.

a. _____ Sriram wanted to match her skills and interests to opportunities in the market.

b. _____ She realized she could use her knowledge to find a way to make "clean" seafood.

c. _____ She advises other potential entrepreneurs to pursue their dreams.

d. _____ She wanted to become an entrepreneur because she wasn't satisfied with her job.

e. _____ She got a lot of help and support from her colleagues and employees.

f. _____ Shiok Meats successfully introduced "clean" shrimp.

g. _____ The rising popularity and decreasing supply of seafood have made its future uncertain.

C DETAILS Write the correct paragraph number (3–6) where each extra detail would fit best.

a. _____ Currently, plant-based seafood is only 1 percent of the plant-based meat market.

b. _____ Sriram likes to give advice to entrepreneurs who are just starting out.

c. _____ The average person eats twice as much seafood as 50 years ago.

d. _____ At $5,000 per kilo, "clean" shrimp is expensive—but the price is coming down.

D Highlight evidence in the reading to support these claims about entrepreneurs. Discuss your answers with a partner.

1. Entrepreneurs start more than one business. (paragraphs 1 and 5)
2. They often have a business education. (paragraph 2)
3. They start businesses that disrupt markets. (paragraph 4)
4. They start businesses in a high-tech field. (paragraph 5)
5. They need money from investors in order to start their businesses. (paragraph 5)

CRITICAL THINKING   Apply knowledge

When you learn new information about a topic, apply or use that knowledge to question and confirm any preexisting ideas. Applying knowledge may strengthen your conclusions, or it may force you to rethink them. For example, if you assumed that all entrepreneurs went to business school, learning about those who did not might make you reconsider your assumption.

REFLECT   Draw conclusions about entrepreneurs.

Think of an entrepreneur that you know or research one on the Internet. Check (✓) the characteristics that are true for that person. Put a *?* if you don't know. Then answer the questions in a small group.

Entrepreneur's name: _____

_____ took risks

_____ disrupted markets

_____ got money from investors

_____ failed before he or she succeeded

_____ started more than one business

_____ is in a high-tech field

_____ has a business education

1. Do your entrepreneurs have a similar profile to Andrés Gutiérrez and Sandhya Sriram?
2. What conclusions can you draw, if any, about entrepreneurs in general?

WRITE

Write an analysis essay about what makes entrepreneurs successful.

You are going to write an essay in response to the question, "What factors make entrepreneurs successful?" Use the ideas, vocabulary, and skills from the unit.

A MODEL Read the essay in response to the question, "What factors make athletes successful?" Underline the factors.

What Factors Make Athletes Successful?

1   It's always interesting and exciting to watch sports, but watching a really great athlete is inspiring. What distinguishes them from other good athletes? You might think it is talent and ability, but both good and great athletes have that. Most superior athletes also have other qualities that help them rise to the highest levels.

2   All exceptional athletes have a strong desire to succeed, and this usually starts at a young age. They set goals and then do everything necessary to reach them. Some of the best examples of this characteristic are long-distance racers. Haile Gebrselassie, a world-famous Ethiopian runner, started running against his father's wishes. In 1988, when he was 15, he lied to his father about entering a marathon. He had no proper equipment but still completed the race in 2 hours and 48 seconds. "I ran in street shoes with plastic soles. They were full of blood," Gebrselassie said in an interview. He went on to win two gold medals in the Olympics in 1996 and 2000.

3   Top athletes do not give up even after serious setbacks. They have the mental strength that helps them come back and perform at an even higher level. Kipchoge Keino, a Kenyan long-distance runner, experienced several problems at the Mexico City Olympics in 1968. He was suffering from gallstones, a dangerous and painful medical condition, but he ran in the 10,000-meter race anyway. He was barely able to finish the race. His doctor advised him that continuing to race would be a danger to his health. Yet, two days later, Keino ran in the 5,000-meter race and won a silver medal. He also won the 1,500-meter race but after even more setbacks. Tired from the earlier race, he decided to sleep an extra hour. He took a later bus, but it got stuck in traffic. So, Keino got off the bus and ran the remaining two miles to the start of the race. In spite of these problems, he still won the gold medal.

4   Finally, the best athletes have great focus and discipline. They are willing to practice for hours, even when it is difficult, boring, and painful. Tatyana McFadden, a para-athlete, races in a

wheelchair. Born in Russia, she has been paralyzed from the waist down since birth. She came to the United States at the age of four. McFadden started serious training and racing when she was just eight years old. Since then, she has done intense daily workouts for her upper body, heart, and lungs, which even athletes who have the full use of their legs find difficult. This training program has been essential in her long and successful athletic career.

5   All of these athletes share a strong desire to win, and they do whatever it takes to reach their goals. Their commitment requires intense training and the ability to overcome setbacks, a process that can make them even stronger and faster. Talent is where these athletes begin, but it is their strength and determination that takes them to the top.

B ANALYZE THE MODEL Answer the questions.

1. The introduction states that good athletes and great athletes start with something in common. What is it? _____

2. What characteristic does each body paragraph describe, and what examples and evidence does the writer provide? Complete the chart.

Characteristic of successful athlete	Name of athlete	Evidence from the model essay

Tatyana McFadden competing in the IPC World Para Athletics Championships

WRITING SKILL   Paraphrase original sources

When you use information in your essay from an original source, such as a website or a book, it's important to present the information in your own words. If you copy the wording from an original source, it's called **plagiarism**, which is not permitted in academic settings. One way to avoid plagiarism is to paraphrase. **Paraphrasing** means changing the words and sentence structure of the original material while still keeping the same meaning. Follow these steps to successfully paraphrase.

1. Underline or highlight key words in the original source.

2. Replace key words with synonyms or phrases that have the same meaning.

3. Change parts of speech (e.g., verbs into nouns, nouns into adjectives).

4. Change the structure of the original source by breaking up the sentences and putting them back together in a different order.

5. Do not add any new information.

6. If you still have some longer parts that are the same as the original, use quotation marks around those parts.

C APPLY Read the excerpt from the model essay and the three paraphrases. Write *1* if the paraphrase is good, *2* if the paraphrase is too similar to the source, and *3* if the paraphrase adds information.

Excerpt from model: What distinguishes [great athletes] from other good athletes? You might think it is talent and ability, but both good and great athletes have that. Most superior athletes also have other qualities that help them rise to the highest levels.

a. _____ **Paraphrase 1:** What makes great athletes different from good athletes? Maybe you think they have talent and ability, which they do have. However, most of them have other characteristics that help them reach the top level of their sport.

b. _____ **Paraphrase 2:** All great athletes have talent and ability, but the best athletes also have a lot of self-confidence and determination.

c. _____ **Paraphrase 3:** All good athletes are talented, but there are some other specific characteristics that mark the difference between good athletes and exceptional ones.

D APPLY Read the original source and the paraphrase used in the model. With a partner, discuss these questions: How did the writer paraphrase the underlined words? What other changes did the writer make?

1. **Original source:** Great athletes demonstrate their hunger for success when they are quite young.

   Paraphrase in model: All exceptional athletes have a strong desire to succeed, and this usually starts at a young age.

2. **Original source:** To be successful, <u>top athletes</u> <u>practice with great concentration and consistency</u>. It's not always fun, but they recognize that it is necessary.

   Paraphrase in model: The best athletes have great focus and discipline. They are willing to practice for hours, even when it is difficult, boring, and painful.

E APPLY In your notebook, paraphrase these sentences from the model essay. Then compare your paraphrases with a partner.

1. Haile Gebrselassie, a world-famous Ethiopian runner, started running against his father's wishes. In 1988, when he was 15, he lied to his father about entering a marathon.

2. [Keino's] doctor advised him that continuing to race would be a danger to his health. Yet, two days later, Keino ran in the 5,000-meter race and won a silver medal.

3. McFadden started serious training and racing when she was just eight years old. Since then, she has done intense daily workouts for her upper body, heart, and lungs, which even athletes with the full use of their legs find difficult.

GRAMMAR Reduced non-essential adjective clauses

A non-essential adjective clause gives additional information about a noun. You can remove it and the sentence will still make sense. Only use the relative pronouns *which* and *who* with non-essential adjective clauses, and set the clause off with commas.

> *Tappsi,* **which was founded in 2012**, *merged with another company in 2015.*

A **non-essential adjective clause** with *be* can be **reduced** (or shortened) by deleting *be* and the relative pronoun. Reducing adjective clauses increases sentence variety and makes your writing more natural.

▶ You can reduce adjective clauses that have passive verb forms (***be* + past participle)**.

> *Tappsi,* ~~*which was*~~ **founded in 2012**, *merged with another company in 2015.*

These reduced clauses are often placed in front of the subject, using a comma.

> ***Founded in 2012***, *Tappsi merged with another company in 2015.*

▶ You can also reduce adjective clauses that contain ***be* + noun**.

> *Sandhya Sriram,* ~~*who is*~~ **a cell biologist**, *was able to grow shrimp in a lab.*

F GRAMMAR Underline four examples of reduced adjective clauses in paragraphs 2 and 3 of the model essay. In your notebook, rewrite each one into a full clause with *be*.

G GRAMMAR Rewrite these sentences in your notebook. Reduce the adjective clause. Move any participle (-*ed*) forms in front of the subject.

1. Kipchoge, who is admired all over the world, retired in 1973.
2. Shiok Meats, which is supported partly by the government, will offer products to the public in just a few years.
3. Andrés Gutiérrez, who is an entrepreneur from Colombia, has received a major new round of funding.
4. Sriram, who is motivated by a strong desire to make the world a better place, started her company with a dream.
5. Shiok Meats, which is funded by several big investors, has a bright future.
6. Gutiérrez's grandmother, who is a farm owner in Colombia, helped him get started.

H EDIT Read the paragraph and notice the bold words. Reduce the two adjective clauses, and correct the three reduced clauses that are incorrect.

Entrepreneur Jeff Bezos

Former Amazon CEO Jeff Bezos, who is the richest person in the world, has a net worth that is about $150 billion. **Bezos born in Albuquerque, New Mexico,** graduated from Princeton University with a degree in electrical engineering. He wrote the business plan for Amazon on a trip from New York to Seattle, and then his parents invested $300,000 to get the company started. **Amazon was originally planned as just a book company** quickly expanded to other products and services. The business, which today is the world's largest online sales company, did about $90 billion of sales in 2019. In 1993, Bezos bought the *Washington Post*, **which was a troubled newspaper at the time. Rescued by Bezos the *Post*** has become another of his success stories.

Books people want to read

Jeff Bezos

PLAN & WRITE

I **BRAINSTORM** Work in a small group and answer the questions.

1. Think of the entrepreneurs you've read about and discussed in this unit. Which three factors below do you think are most responsible for their success? Add other success factors that you think are important.

   a. Have a business education

   b. Take risks

   c. Have natural talent and ability

   d. Disrupt markets

   e. Have a lot of investors

   f. Fail before they succeed

   g. Start more than one business

   h. Are in a high-tech field

   i. _____

   j. _____

2. Complete the chart with evidence to support your claim that the three factors are important for an entrepreneur's success. Use information from the Reflect activities or do some research on other entrepreneurs.

Success factor	Evidence from Andrés Gutiérrez article	Evidence from Sandhya Sriram article	Evidence from other entrepreneurs

WRITING TIP

When you do research online or in books, don't read everything. Read with a purpose: What is relevant for your writing task? For example, for the assignment, "What factors make entrepreneurs successful?" look for information that relates to the factors you have chosen. When you find relevant information, take notes, paraphrasing any important information you plan to use in your essay.

J OUTLINE Complete the outline using information from activity I.

Introductory paragraph

Background information: _____

_____

Thesis statement: _____

_____

Body paragraphs

Two to three factors responsible for an entrepreneur's success:

_____

_____

_____

Entrepreneur's experiences and achievements as supporting evidence:

_____

_____

_____

Concluding paragraph

Final comment: _____

_____

K FIRST DRAFT Use your outline to write a first draft of your essay.

L REVISE Use this list as you write your second draft.

- ☐ Will your introduction catch the reader's attention?
- ☐ Does your thesis statement clearly express your claims about the factors for success?
- ☐ Do your body paragraphs adequately describe those factors?
- ☐ Do your body paragraphs provide enough evidence to support your claims?
- ☐ Does your conclusion make a comment or prediction about the success of entrepreneurs?

M EDIT Use this list as you write your final draft.

- ☐ Did you use paraphrases that are sufficiently different from the original sources?
- ☐ Did you reduce adjective clauses appropriately?
- ☐ Did you use commas in non-essential adjective clauses?

N FINAL DRAFT Reread your essay and correct any errors. Then submit it to your teacher.

REFLECT

A Check (✓) the Reflect activities you can do and the academic skills you can use.

- ☐ compare types of businesses
- ☐ interpret a pie chart about businesses
- ☐ relate data to a business opportunity
- ☐ draw conclusions about entrepreneurs
- ☐ write an analysis essay about what makes entrepreneurs successful

- ☐ find evidence
- ☐ paraphrase original sources
- ☐ reduced non-essential adjective clauses
- ☐ apply knowledge

B Write the vocabulary words from the unit in the correct column. Add any other words that you learned. Circle words you still need to practice.

NOUN	VERB	ADJECTIVE	ADVERB & OTHER

C Reflect on the ideas in the unit as you answer these questions.

1. Do you know anyone who has the characteristics to make him or her a successful entrepreneur? Describe him or her.

2. Does what you learned in the unit make you want to become an entrepreneur? Explain.

3. What is the most important thing you learned in this unit?

SHARING A LAUGH

Yosakoi dancers enjoy another dance team's performance in Kumamoto, Japan.

IN THIS UNIT

▶ Consider why we laugh

▶ Analyze different kinds of laughter

▶ Assess statements about laughter

▶ Evaluate research claims about laughter

▶ Write a research report about laughter

SKILLS

READING
Understand pronoun references

WRITING
Summarize research for a research report

GRAMMAR
Noun modifiers

CRITICAL THINKING
Evaluate research claims

▶ ## CONNECT TO THE TOPIC

1. Look at the photo. How does it make you feel?

2. Do you think that animals can laugh?

Emily and Rishi, an orangutan, play together in Miami, Florida, USA.

LAUGHTER ACROSS SPECIES

A PREDICT Read the title and look at the photo. What do you think the video is about? Then watch the video and check your prediction. ▶ 5.1

B Watch the video. Check (✓) the ideas that are discussed in the video about humans and other animals. ▶ 5.1

Humans

1. _____ Babies learn to laugh from their parents.

2. _____ Laughter is a natural human behavior.

3. _____ Babies spend more time laughing than crying.

4. _____ Simple games often make babies laugh.

5. _____ Laughter helps build relationships between babies and their parents.

Other animals

1. _____ Many other animals, including dogs and cats, laugh.

2. _____ Monkeys that live in zoos laugh more than monkeys that live in the wild.

3. _____ Chimpanzees and gorillas laugh when they are tickled.

4. _____ The sound of human and primate laughter is different.

5. _____ Laughter is a natural part of play for both humans and primates.

PREPARE TO READ

A VOCABULARY Read the definitions. Complete the paragraph with the correct form of the words. Three words are extra.

---

contagious (adj) easily spread from one person to another

distinguish (v) to recognize or understand the difference between two things

emerge (v) to come out or start to develop

engage in (v phr) to take part in

evolve (v) to change slowly over time

industrialized (adj) describing places with well-developed manufacturing

innate (adj) natural from birth

origin (n) the beginning or cause of something

primarily (adv) mainly

threatening (adj) showing the possibility that something bad will happen

---

Happiness is often connected to our well-being—how healthy we are. Unfortunately, getting sick is part of being human. Medical experts [1]_____ between two types of diseases: infectious and noninfectious. Some infectious diseases, such as malaria, are carried by insects. These insects [2]_____ over millions of years to bite humans and eat their blood, which spreads the disease. In most [3]_____ countries, however, it is [4]_____ noninfectious diseases that affect the largest number of people. For many years, the [5]_____ of these diseases was a mystery, but today we understand them better. A combination of [6]_____ factors, such as your genes, and lifestyle choices can cause these diseases. Sadly, in recent years, noninfectious diseases [7]_____ as a major problem in less industrialized nations as well.

B PERSONALIZE Discuss these questions with a partner.

1. Do you think laughter is an **innate** behavior or something we learn to do?
2. What human feelings or behavior do you think are **contagious**?
3. Can you **distinguish** between real and fake laughter?

REFLECT   Consider why we laugh.

You are going to read about the origins of human laughter. Check (✓) the three most common times you think people laugh. Then discuss your ideas with a partner.

We laugh most when we . . .

_____ think something is funny.

_____ are angry.

_____ are uncomfortable.

_____ are happy.

_____ want to show that we understand.

_____ want to show that we are listening.

_____ want to show that we are friendly.

_____ want to interrupt someone.

THE ORIGINS OF
LAUGHTER

A PREDICT Read the first paragraph. Check (✓) the three topics that you think the article will discuss.

1. _____ Laughter in other animals
2. _____ Why some people are funny
3. _____ How laughter affects health
4. _____ The history of laughter
5. _____ The function of laughter

1   Take some time to watch people laugh—really laugh. They make unusual sounds, they can't catch their breath, they can't speak, and they curl their bodies into strange shapes. If you had never seen anyone laugh before, this would look and sound quite strange, perhaps even frightening. Yet laughter is a universal human activity. Everyone does it and they have been doing it throughout history. But are humans the only species that laughs? Where did this strange behavior come from? And why do we do it?

2   First of all, we are not the only species that laughs. Most primates[1], including chimpanzees and gorillas, **engage in** some form of laughter, though it does not sound like human laughter. Their laughter is easiest to see and hear if a person or another animal tickles them. Young chimps, especially males, participate in playful fighting that often includes tickling. Scientists believe that chimp "laughter" may be a way to show that the activity is just for fun and not **threatening**. So, what do these animals and humans have in common?

3   To answer this question, we need to consider the **origins** of laughter. Most scientists agree that laughter has been a part of social relationships from the very beginning. It probably **emerged** at about the time that humans began to live in larger social groups. <u>This</u> may also explain why we find laughter among other species that live in groups, such as gorillas and chimpanzees. Marine biologists believe that even dolphins, which are also social animals, display something like laughter.

4   Scientists are also interested in the characteristics of different kinds of laughter. One influential theory was proposed by Matthew Gervais and David Sloan Wilson. They believe there are actually two types of laughter, and these emerged at different times in human history. The first kind of laughter may have emerged as early as 4 million years ago, probably before speech. This laughter is an **innate** behavior; you don't have to learn to do it. It is also involuntary; in other words, you cannot plan it or easily control it. It just happens, like when someone tickles you. Finally, it can be **contagious**. You are more likely to laugh when you hear someone else laugh.

5   Robert Provine, an expert on laughter, believes that involuntary laughter kept—and still keeps—social relationships positive and friendly in social groups. Laughter is a signal that says, "We are all friends; there is no trouble here." This helped groups to live without conflicts and to cooperate in finding food and protecting the whole group. And because this laughter is an involuntary behavior, these early humans did not have to think about it or plan it.

6   The second type of laughter—voluntary laughter—emerged later, probably about 2 million years ago, according to Gervais and Wilson. Unlike involuntary laughter, it is under our control and sounds almost, but not exactly, the same. Why have humans developed two kinds of laughter that sound almost alike? Gervais and Wilson believe that voluntary laughter takes advantage of the effects of involuntary laughter. In other words, people often laugh deliberately because they know that it keeps social relationships peaceful. Interestingly, chimpanzees also engage in voluntary laughter for similar reasons.

Two friends share a laugh in the USA.

[1]**primate** (n) a member of the most developed and intelligent group of mammals

7   Although these two types of laughter sound similar, we are able to recognize the difference; voluntary laughter sounds a bit fake. Perhaps because both types of laughter **evolved** in early humans, this is true across cultures. In brain scans of people listening to laughter, different areas of the brain light up depending on which kind they hear. Scientist Greg Bryant played very short recordings of both types to people all over the world, and participants were able to guess the difference most of the time. Not only were listeners in his study able to **distinguish** between voluntary and involuntary laughter, but they could also distinguish laughter among friends from laughter among strangers. This ability to distinguish also extended across cultures. A Hadza hunter-gatherer[2] in Tanzania, for example, could immediately tell that two young women in California were friends after listening to one second of their laughter.

8   Bryant found, though, that age and location of participants affected how easily they could distinguish between voluntary and involuntary laughter. People from smaller, less **industrialized** regions were generally better at this task. Bryant believes that people in these communities are more dependent on social relationships than those who live in more industrialized countries. Therefore, they may be more sensitive to these differences. He also found that young children are less able to distinguish between the two types of laughter, but their ability improves as they grow up and participate more in a community's social life.

9   For more than 4 million years, laughter has been **primarily** a social activity. Both types of laughter, involuntary and voluntary, have helped to maintain peace and cooperation among humans and other social species.

---

[2]**hunter-gatherer** (n) a member of a group of people that hunts and collects food instead of farming

An Afar woman laughing, Ethiopia

B MAIN IDEAS Highlight the main ideas in paragraphs 2–8. Then complete the sentence about the main idea of the reading.

Laughter has a primarily _____ function.

C DETAILS Check (✓) the correct researcher(s) for each statement. Two statements are not connected to any researcher.

	Provine	Gervais & Wilson	Bryant
1. Two types of laughter probably emerged about 2 million years apart.			
2. Laughter improves social relationships.			
3. Humans can hear the difference between involuntary and voluntary laughter.			
4. Laughter may have emerged as the size of social groups increased.			
5. Voluntary laughter uses the positive effects of involuntary laughter.			
6. Humans can distinguish between laughter among friends and among strangers.			
7. Dolphins also have a form of laughter.			
8. Adults are better than children at distinguishing between types of laughter.			

D DETAILS Read each statement. Write T for *True*, F for *False*, or NG for *Not Given* based on the information in the article.

1. _____ Chimpanzee laughter sounds very similar to human laughter.

2. _____ Scientists believe that laughter used to be a threatening signal.

3. _____ Humans were probably laughing before they were speaking.

4. _____ Tickling results in voluntary laughter.

5. _____ Women can better distinguish between the two types of laughter than men.

6. _____ The brain responds differently to voluntary and involuntary laughter.

7. _____ Children are not as good as adults at distinguishing between the two types of laughter.

8. _____ Hunter-gatherers are better than most people at distinguishing between types of laughter.

READING SKILL   Understand pronoun references

The pronouns *this*, *that*, *these*, and *those* are used to refer back to nouns, noun phrases, or whole ideas. When you see these pronouns, look back at the previous sentence or sentences to see what is being referred to. In these examples, the pronoun is in bold and the noun phrase or idea it refers to is underlined.

> *Researchers did <u>a series of studies to determine the effect of different types of exercise on hunger</u>. **These** have provided important information about the role of exercise in weight control.*

> *In a series of studies, researchers found that <u>exercise decreased hunger</u>. **This** suggests that exercise plays a more important role in controlling weight than previously thought.*

E APPLY In the article *The Origins of Laughter*, what does *this* refer to in sentence 4 of paragraph 3?

   a. . . . humans began to live in larger social groups.

   b. It probably emerged at about the time that humans began to live in larger social groups.

   c. . . . laughter has been part of social relationships from the very beginning.

F APPLY Find these pronouns in the article. Circle the noun, noun phrase, or idea that each bold word refers to.

   1. **this** would look and sound quite strange (paragraph 1)

   2. and **these** emerged at different times (paragraph 4)

   3. **This** helped groups to live without conflicts (paragraph 5)

   4. **this** is true across cultures (paragraph 7)

   5. **those** who live in more industrialized countries (paragraph 8)

REFLECT   Analyze different kinds of laughter.

Check (✓) whether each situation is an example of voluntary laughter or involuntary laughter. In some cases, you may check both. Explain your reasons to a partner.

	Voluntary	Involuntary
1. A child laughs when she is tickled.		
2. An employee laughs when his boss tells a bad joke.		
3. You laugh as you are talking with a group of people you just met.		
4. A group of teenagers laugh as they watch an online video.		

PREPARE TO READ

A VOCABULARY Read the sentences. Choose the correct meaning for the words in bold.

1. Many people love watching online videos of kittens because kittens are so **adorable**.

   a. popular   b. small   c. lovable

2. It was immediately **apparent** that the show wasn't funny. The first joke was awful.

   a. clear   b. surprising   c. uncomfortable

3. It's reasonable to **assume** that people tell the truth most of the time. It's fairly normal.

   a. think something is   b. question or wonder   c. believe something
   true without proof   that is false

4. Experts believe that the **bond** between identical twins is especially strong.

   a. language   b. thought   c. connection

5. Some people send unpleasant messages online to **bully** other people they don't like.

   a. play with   b. work with   c. scare and threaten

6. There were several **episodes** of violence in the city last night. One involved a fight at a park.

   a. discussions   b. events   c. places

7. Seeing something **humorous**, such as a comedy, usually makes people laugh.

   a. creative   b. unusual   c. funny

8. Many Hollywood movies have no important message. They are **purely** for entertainment.

   a. especially   b. completely   c. certainly

9. Her brothers always **teased** her about being the youngest. She didn't like it.

   a. made fun of   b. worked with   c. talked to

10. Even a well-planned trip can **turn out** to be a disaster if the weather is bad.

    a. change for the better   b. occur in the wrong way   c. happen; end up

---

REFLECT   Assess statements about laughter.

Before reading about more research on laughter, consider the following statements, which many people believe are true. What do you think? Choose T for *True* or F for *False*. Explain your reasons in a small group.

QUIZ

FACTS ABOUT LAUGHTER?

1.	Laughing for 15 minutes burns 50 calories.	T	F
2.	Adults laugh about 15 times a day.	T	F
3.	Children laugh about 300 times a day.	T	F
4.	Laughter reduces pain.	T	F
5.	You can't make yourself laugh by tickling yourself.	T	F
6.	Birds have a form of laughter.	T	F

WHY WE LAUGH

A PREDICT Skim the article. Check (✓) the three topics you think the article will discuss. Confirm your answers after you read.

1. _____ When people laugh
2. _____ What makes something funny
3. _____ Differences in when men and women laugh
4. _____ Differences in laughter across ages
5. _____ The function of laughter

A father and son visit the Caspian Sea.

5.2

1   Why do we laugh? Surprisingly, it's not just because we hear something funny. How and when we laugh may depend on where we are, what we are doing, and who we are with—but most of the time, it is not related to anything **humorous**. Indeed, just as for early humans, today, most laughter has a **purely** social function.

2   We know a lot about laughter, in part, because of the research of Robert Provine. He had an unusual but effective way of collecting data. He and his students sat in cafes, shopping malls, schools, and parks near his home in the United States. They secretly watched and listened to people having conversations. They were especially interested in what Provine calls "laughter **episodes**." Every time he and his students heard a laughter episode, they took notes about who laughed and when.

3   Before doing this research, like most of us, Provine had **assumed** that whatever was said before the laugh (the *pre-laugh comment*) would be something funny. Surprisingly, most people laughed at very ordinary comments or questions. For example, "I'll see you later," "There you go!" or "Are you sure?" After listening to and studying hundreds of these episodes, he estimated that between 80 and 90 percent of laughter is social. He concluded that like the laughter that evolved among early humans, people today use laughter to form and strengthen social **bonds**.

4   When Provine began to look closely at his data, he found interesting patterns in who laughed most and when they laughed. He discovered that the person who made the pre-laugh comment laughed much more often than the listener. Provine also analyzed his data to find out whether there were any differences between men and women in the patterns of laughter. It soon became **apparent** that there were. The data in Table 1 clearly shows that men get more laughs than women. Provine suggested one possible explanation for this. Women are more likely to want to please others, so they use laughter to send a positive signal about relationships more often than men do.

How often do men and women laugh?				
Gender of speaker	Gender of listener	Number of laughter episodes	Times speaker laughs	Times listener laughs
Male	Male	275	75.6%	60%
Female	Female	502	86%	49.8%
Male	Female	238	66%	71%
Female	Male	185	88.1%	38.9%

Table 1   **Source:** Provine, R. (1993)

5   Laughter plays a significant role in relationships. It is important for parents and babies. It's easy to make a baby laugh, and a baby's laughter generally brings parents great joy. A simple game of peekaboo[1] can send babies into **adorable** giggles. These laughing episodes are enjoyable for both parents and babies, but they also have a function: They create a strong bond between parent and child. Laughing can have a positive impact on other family relationships, too. Recent research has indicated that couples who are able to laugh together during stressful situations are more likely to have longer and happier marriages.

6   What about the laughter that is in response to something that is actually funny? Although Provine's research shows most laughter is not in response to anything humorous, of course, we do laugh at funny things. Yet, even this kind of laughter **turns out** to be social. Think about it. How often do you laugh when you are alone, even when something is funny? Probably not very often. Scientists who study laughter soon realized that the best way to make their research participants laugh was to study them in pairs or groups. Even the best jokes rarely made participants laugh if they were alone. In fact, you are 30 times more likely to laugh when you are in the company of others than when you are by yourself. Even if you are laughing about something funny, perhaps as you watch a movie, your response is also a signal to others that you are enjoying yourself and an invitation to join you in the fun. Perhaps this is why we are more likely to laugh with friends than with strangers and also why laughter is often contagious.

7   Laughter is clearly powerful, but that power can also be used in negative ways. When you laugh *with* other people, you are expressing friendship. What about when you laugh *at* other people? With friends, this could be just gentle **teasing**. However, it can also be a way to show others that you think you are better than they are. This kind of laughter can be especially unkind when several people laugh together at another person. Then it can become a form of **bullying**.

8   Some functions of laughter are universal while others may be more culturally specific. But in all cases, laughter is about relationships between people, and it should be understood as social behavior.

---

[1]**peekaboo** (n) a game played with babies and small children in which you cover your face with your hands and then quickly take them away and say "Peekaboo!"

B MAIN IDEAS Highlight the main ideas in paragraphs 2–7. Then write one sentence expressing the main idea of the whole article.

_____

C DETAILS Look at Table 1. Then complete each sentence with the word *men* or *women*.

1. Men laughed more when listening to _____.

2. Women laughed more when listening to _____.

3. Men laughed more when speaking to _____.

4. Among the people in the study, speakers who were _____ laughed the most.

D DETAILS Are these statements in the article? If so, how are they referred to? Write *a*, *b*, or *c* for each.

a. not in the article	b. in the article but with no source	c. referred to as the work of Provine

1. _____ Women listeners are more likely to laugh during conversations.

2. _____ People rarely laugh when they are alone.

3. _____ Only about 10–20 percent of all laughter is about something funny.

4. _____ People who live in cities laugh more than people who live in the country.

5. _____ Laughter can help make marriages stronger.

6. _____ Speakers laugh more frequently than listeners.

7. _____ People laugh more in some cultures than in others.

8. _____ We are more likely to laugh among friends.

E Circle the noun phrase or idea that each pronoun refers to in the article.

1. Provine suggested one possible explanation for **this**. (paragraph 4)

2. Perhaps **this** is why we are more likely to laugh with friends than with strangers. (paragraph 6)

3. With friends, **this** could be just gentle teasing. (paragraph 7)

CRITICAL THINKING   Evaluate research claims

Writers often make claims about research to support their ideas. When you read a claim, don't assume it's true—think about *how likely* it is to be true. Some claims exaggerate the results of research, take them out of context, or are just wrong. For example, if a study found that women laughed after men's comments more than men laughed after women's comments, this does not support the claim that men are funnier than women. The women may have laughed for many different reasons, not just because the men were funny.

REFLECT   Evaluate research claims about laughter.

Read the results of two research studies. Underline the claim made by each writer. With a partner, consider the research and discuss a better claim.

1. In this study, participants over the age of 70 watched short videos. Some were funny; others were not. The participants remembered the funny ones the best. This shows that humorous content helps older people improve their memory.

2. In a study, some participants watched a humorous television program alone, and others watched the same program in pairs. The pairs laughed more than the participants who watched alone. This shows that laughter increases as the size of the group increases.

WRITE

You are going to collect data about when and why you laugh. You will write a report to summarize the research described in the article *Why We Laugh* and compare that information to the results of your research. Use the ideas, vocabulary, and skills from the unit.

A MODEL Read the model report. Discuss these questions with a partner.

1. What is the goal of the new research? What information will it add to our knowledge of laughter?
2. Do the results confirm previous research?

Research Report on Age and Laughter

Introduction

1   Laughter is a common form of social behavior, but it is also very individual. If you listen, you quickly notice that everyone has a different laugh. However, research done in the past 30 years suggests that we all recognize different types of human laughter.

Summary of previous research

2   The article *The Origins of Laughter* discusses the origins of human laughter. Research by Robert Provine suggests that all laughter promotes social bonds. Studies by Matthew Gervais and David Sloan Wilson show that there are two types of laughter, involuntary and voluntary. Involuntary laughter is automatic, whereas voluntary laughter can be controlled. Even though they sound similar, our brains can tell the difference. One study by Greg Bryant demonstrates that people from all cultures can tell the difference. However, he found that adults are better able to judge the difference than children. Additionally, people from less industrialized communities are better at hearing the difference than those from more industrialized ones. The article concludes that laughing has always had a social function.

Purpose of current research

3   The new research described here will show how age affects our ability to distinguish between involuntary and voluntary laughter. Although other studies have researched the impact of age, they did not include participants older than 40. This research will add to our knowledge of this topic and show in more detail how this ability changes with age.

Research procedures

4   This research included 40 people: 22 women and 18 men from age 10 to 63. The research began with an explanation of the difference between the two types of laughter. The participants

listened to one example of each type of laughter to make sure that they understood the difference. Then they listened to 10 short recordings of involuntary and voluntary laughter. These were the same recordings used in the study reviewed in *The Origins of Laughter*. After listening to each recording, participants marked a chart. They wrote if they thought the laughter was involuntary or voluntary.

Results and discussion

5   The results show that older listeners were more accurate than younger participants. The results also show that accuracy increased with age. The age 40–49 group was the most accurate at 90 percent, and the age 10–15 group was the least accurate at 40 percent. There was a steady increase in accuracy with age, except in the oldest group. The age 50–63 group had an accuracy rate of 78 percent. These results are not surprising. Previous research suggests that voluntary laughter is learned behavior. So it makes sense that the ability to distinguish between the two types of laughter is also learned over time. The decline in accuracy in the oldest group could be because hearing generally gets worse with age.

Conclusion

6   The results of the research show that age affects our ability to distinguish types of laughter. However, there are limits to this new research. It is based on a small number of participants. Future research should include more participants, as well as participants older than 63.

B ANALYZE THE MODEL What information is included in each section of the report? Write the correct heading number (1–6) next to the information.

1. Introduction	3. Purpose of current research	5. Results and discussion
2. Summary of previous research	4. Research procedures	6. Conclusion

a. _____ a description of the participants

b. _____ results of previous studies

c. _____ a comparison of current results to previous results

d. _____ general background information about laughter

e. _____ a description of how the study was done

f. _____ an explanation of problems in past research

g. _____ an interpretation of what the results might mean

h. _____ suggestions for future research

i. _____ definitions of involuntary and voluntary laughter

j. _____ a statement of the goals of the current study

Nuuk, Greenland

WRITING SKILL   Summarize research for a research report

A summary is a short piece of writing that presents the main points of another text. A summary is much shorter than the original text and is written in the writer's own words.

In a research report, you first include a summary of previous research that is relevant to your new research. Follow these steps to summarize previous research:

1. Read the original text and make sure you understand it.
2. Find the paragraphs that are relevant to your research. Highlight the main ideas in these paragraphs.
3. The first sentence of your summary should include a reference to the original text (e.g., the title, date, and author if known) and explain what the text is mostly about.
4. Paraphrase the main ideas from step 2 in your own words (see the Writing Skill in Unit 4).
5. Don't include supporting details from the original text in your summary.
6. Finish your summary with a sentence about what we can conclude from the research.

C APPLY Review the article *The Origins of Laughter* and the "Summary of previous research" in the model research report. Follow these steps.

1. In the summary of previous research, highlight the reference to the article. Underline what the writer says the article is mostly about.

2. Where does the information summarized in the model appear in the article *The Origins of Laughter*? Write the five paragraph numbers where the information comes from.

   _____

3. Underline the sentence in the summary that states what we can conclude from the research.

D APPLY For your research report, you will summarize the research in the article *Why We Laugh*. Review the article and follow these steps.

1. Which paragraphs in the article are mostly about Robert Provine's research? Write the four paragraph numbers. _____

2. Review the main ideas you highlighted in these paragraphs.

3. Use those main ideas to complete the summary of previous research. Use these sentence starters to help you.

    The article *Why We Laugh* discusses _____.

    The author focuses on the research of _____, who listened to _____.

    He was surprised to find out that most laughter _____.

    He also found some interesting patterns: _____

    _____.

    Finally, he found that even when something is funny _____

    _____.

    From the article, we can conclude that _____

    _____.

GRAMMAR Noun modifiers

One way to describe or modify nouns is with adjectives. An adjective usually comes before the noun it modifies. However, you can also include **noun modifiers** after a noun. This is helpful in academic writing because it allows you to communicate a lot of information in a few words. Notice these noun modifiers.

Participial phrases

> The audience learned about a research <u>project</u> **starting next year**.

> The <u>research</u> **done on laughter in the 1990s** is a useful place to begin.

Prepositional phrases

> The lecturer discussed <u>research</u> **about different types of laughter**.

> The <u>results</u> **of the survey** will surprise everyone.

Infinitive phrases

> There is no <u>reason</u> **to doubt the results of the research**.

> Everyone has the <u>ability</u> **to distinguish between different kinds of laughter**.

E GRAMMAR Highlight examples of nouns + noun modifiers in the model.

1. Paragraph 1: one noun + participial phrase

2. Paragraph 2: two nouns + prepositional phrases

3. Paragraph 3: one noun + infinitive phrase, one noun + participial phrase

4. Paragraph 4: one noun + participial phrase

F GRAMMAR Complete the sentences with different types of noun modifiers.

1. Researchers listened to laughter _____.

2. Provine observed people _____.

3. What's the most important quality _____?

4. The results _____ will change the field.

5. Laughter is a great way _____.

6. I usually laugh when I hear a joke _____.

7. I am interested in articles _____.

8. I had the opportunity _____.

PLAN & WRITE

G RESEARCH For a short period of time (for example, two days), record your laughter episodes. Follow the steps below.

1. Complete the chart every time you laugh.

Type of laughter episode	Number of times (I, II, III, IIII, IIII)	Notes (e.g., who were you talking to, who said something funny, what did they say?)
1. I laughed just after I said something.		
2. I laughed just after someone else said something.		
3. I laughed watching, listening to, or reading something alone.		
4. I laughed watching, listening to, or reading something with others.		

2. Add up the total number of laughter episodes. _____

3. Calculate the percentage of laughter episodes in each of the four types.

   Type 1: _____   Type 2: _____   Type 3: _____   Type 4: _____

H PLAN Share the results from your research in a small group. Then answer the questions.

1. In what situations did you laugh the most and the least frequently?

2. Review your notes column. Do you see any interesting patterns?

3. Look at your summary of the research reported in *Why We Laugh* from activity D. Were your results similar to that research?

4. How do your results add to what we know about laughter? How was your study different from Provine's? Consider the following possibilities:

   ▶ Do you have a different background than the people who Provine studied?

   ▶ Are you from a different culture or country?

   ▶ Are you in a different age group?

   ▶ Does studying your own behavior give you a unique understanding?

I OUTLINE Complete an outline using ideas and details from your summary and your study.

Introduction

Laughter is _____

_____

Summary of previous research

The article *Why We Laugh* discusses _____

_____

Purpose of current research

This study will improve our understanding of laughter by _____

_____

Procedures

In this study, I collected my own laughter episodes over a period of _____

_____

Results and discussion

My results show that I laughed most often when _____

_____

The contrast between my results and previous research may be a result of _____

_____

Conclusion

The results of the research show _____

_____

Because this study had only one subject, _____

_____

J FIRST DRAFT Use your outline to write a first draft of your report.

K REVISE Use this list as you write your second draft.

☐ Does the introduction provide enough information for your reader to understand what your study is about?

☐ Is the summary of the previous research from *Why We Laugh* complete and in your own words?

☐ Do you clearly state the purpose of your current research?

☐ Does the procedures section have enough information for your reader to understand how you conducted your study?

☐ Does your report describe your results and compare them to Provine's?

☐ Is your conclusion based only on your results?

L EDIT Use this list as you write your final draft.

☐ Does your report follow the format for reporting research?

☐ Did you use noun modifiers appropriately?

☐ Did you use the correct verb forms?

M FINAL DRAFT Reread your report and correct any errors. Then submit it to your teacher.

Laughing sculptures by artist Yue Minjun, Beijing, China

REFLECT

A Check (✓) the Reflect activities you can do and the academic skills you can use.

☐ consider why we laugh

☐ analyze different kinds of laughter

☐ assess statements about laughter

☐ evaluate research claims about laughter

☐ write a research report about laughter

☐ understand pronoun references

☐ summarize research for a research report

☐ noun modifiers

☐ evaluate research claims

B Write the vocabulary words from the unit in the correct column. Add any other words that you learned. Circle words you still need to practice.

NOUN	VERB	ADJECTIVE	ADVERB & OTHER

C Reflect on the ideas in the unit as you answer these questions.

1. Now that you understand more about the function of laughter, what have you observed in the laughter among friends, family, and colleagues?

2. What is the most important thing you learned in this unit?

OUR CHANGING CITIES

The Flame Towers seen from the Dağüstü Park, Baku, Azerbaijan

CONNECT TO THE TOPIC

1. Look at the photo. How would you describe this city?

2. Think of a city you know well. How is it different from 50 years ago? How do you think it will change in the next 50 years?

WATCH

Daniel Raven-Ellison walked 1,686 kilometers across all the national parks and cities in the U.K. while wearing a device that tracked his emotions.

THE FIRST
NATIONAL PARK CITY

A You are going to watch a video of National Geographic Explorer Daniel Raven-Ellison talking about a national park. What are national parks, and where are they usually located? Can you describe one? Discuss your ideas with a partner.

B Watch the video. Write T for *True* or F for *False* for each statement. ▶ 6.1

1. _____ London does not have many parks.

2. _____ Daniel Raven-Ellison wants London to be a National Park City.

3. _____ There are about 50,000 species of wildlife in London.

4. _____ When Raven-Ellison started the National Park project, most people thought it was a great idea.

5. _____ London became the first National Park City in 2019.

C Watch again. Check (✓) the three statements that you think Raven-Ellison would agree with. ▶ 6.1

1. _____ It's more important to protect animals in wild areas than in cities.

2. _____ Humans need to have a better relationship with nature.

3. _____ London will probably be the only National Park City.

4. _____ Access to nature will improve human health.

5. _____ Parks can help slow climate change.

PREPARE TO READ

A VOCABULARY Read the sentences and choose the correct meaning for the words in bold.

1. An **aggressive** dog can be frightening and sometimes even dangerous.

   a. large and heavy   b. lonely   c. threatening and unfriendly

2. In normal **circumstances**, lions have between two and six babies every year.

   a. events   b. times of the year   c. conditions

3. **Genes** are partly responsible for how we look and behave.

   a. extended families   b. parts of a cell passed from parent to child   c. lifestyle choices and wellness habits

4. Some animals hide in trees so they can avoid **predators**.

   a. harmful diseases   b. competitors   c. animals that kill other animals

5. The activity of the bacteria appears to be **random**. Researchers cannot find any pattern.

   a. based on science   b. done by chance, not planned   c. dangerous

6. Some people are **suited to** desk jobs, whereas others prefer jobs with more variety.

   a. well matched for   b. qualified for   c. opposed to

7. The **surface** of the lake reflects the sunlight.

   a. top layer   b. quality   c. appearance

8. Male birds of some species threaten other males who come into their **territory**.

   a. family   b. nest   c. area

9. Many wild animals do not **thrive** in zoos. They need to live in the wild.

   a. exist   b. live successfully   c. have babies

10. People with personality **traits** such as generosity and kindness are usually well liked.

    a. characteristics   b. goals   c. descriptions

B PERSONALIZE Discuss these questions with a partner.

1. What kind of place is most **suited to** your personality and lifestyle?
2. What **traits** make this place appealing?
3. Under what **circumstances** do you do your best at school?

REFLECT   Consider how wild animals live in a city.

You are going to read about wild animals that live in urban areas. In a small group, choose one of the wild animals. Discuss the questions.

coyote	deer	fox	hawk	monkey

1. How do you think the animal came to live in the city?
2. How do you think it impacts the city environment?
3. How do you think it impacts human activity?
4. How do you think people feel about the animal's presence in the city?

WILD IN THE CITY

6.1

1   In 2007, half of the world's population was living in cities. By 2050, that figure is expected to be closer to two-thirds. These growing urban centers are spreading into animal habitats and causing significant changes in animals' lives. Although many scientists see this as a negative development—and, indeed, some animals do not survive these changes—surprisingly, many animals **thrive** in urban areas.

2   Many city residents are used to seeing peregrine falcons soaring above them. These birds usually make their homes on the sides of cliffs[1], but they are happy living on top of skyscrapers instead. Some animals are naturally more **suited to** city life because they don't need to change their habits very much. For other species, however, life in the city is more of a challenge. For them, this new habitat requires changes in behavior, but they are still able

[1]**cliff** (n) a high area of rock, often above the ocean

A PREVIEW Which wild animals do you think have the most success in urban areas?

to adapt successfully. For example, foxes normally hunt during the day in the wild, but they have learned to hunt at night in the city to avoid people and cars.

3   Ironically, for some animals, the city is an easier place to live than a wild habitat. There are fewer **predators**, and humans give them greater access to food. Take the crow, for example. Wild crows typically try to open nuts by dropping them on rocks, but some smart city crows let humans help them. In Akita, Japan, crows drop nuts on the ground near a driving school. As student drivers drive over the nuts, the nuts are cracked open. With a less stressful life, many urban animals put more energy into raising larger and more frequent families. For one species of bird, the North American junco, these new **circumstances** have even had an impact on how the birds choose a mate. In the wild, where these birds generally have just one family per year, females prefer **aggressive** males, who can defend their **territory**. However, in the safer city, where juncos have several families a year, females prefer less aggressive males who will help with the babies.

Peregrine falcon, Chicago,
Illinois, USA

4   These changes in behavior are all under the animals' control, but evolution is also hard at work in the city, resulting in more fundamental[2] changes. Evolution is the process by which **random** changes in **genes**, called *mutations*, occur in a species. If a mutation helps the animal to survive, it will be passed to the next generation. This will eventually lead to change across the whole species. For example, one species of lizard in Puerto Rico, called anoles, once lived primarily in the jungle and climbed trees. Since moving to the city, however, they have evolved, gradually developing longer legs and more sticky spots on their feet. Both of these changes help them climb the smoother **surfaces** of the city, like walls and windows. The wing size of cliff swallows has also evolved as a result of human activity. Many swallows with long wings were killed because they could not move out of the way of moving cars. That left birds with shorter wings, which allow them to make quicker turns and avoid traffic. As a result, the genes for short wings have now spread across the entire species.

5   Finally, there are evolutionary changes that we can't see. Since most land animals are unable to cross city roads and highways, their territories have become much smaller. In fact, the territory of some smaller animals may be limited to city parks, leaving them with few choices for mates. Some experts maintain that this is a negative development for species because it reduces gene diversity, and diversity keeps a species strong. However, new research suggests that these smaller gene pools may make it easier for beneficial **traits** to spread. White-footed mice once lived all over the northeastern United States and Canada, but many now live only in city parks. Since the mice can only find mates in their own park, each park's population has evolved in different ways. Scientists who study these mice discovered two specific mutations that have helped one group of mice to survive in New York City. The first mutation helps them process their new food source: the fatty junk food that humans throw away. The second helps protect them from the harmful metals in the city's polluted soil.

6   All of these changes are taking place much faster than expected. Scientists have long believed that evolutionary changes occur over hundreds or thousands of years, but these changes are taking place within a single human generation. It is possible that the main reason for the faster pace of change is today's most powerful force in evolution—human behavior.

---

[2]**fundamental** (adj) related to the most basic and important parts of something

An otter family living in Singapore's Kallang Basin area

B MAIN IDEAS Write the correct paragraph number (2–5) next to its main idea. One idea is extra.

a. _____ An easier life in the city has changed the way some urban animals behave.

b. _____ Animals that interact with humans regularly are changing the most quickly.

c. _____ Genetic changes are happening more quickly because populations are so small.

d. _____ Some animals have changed their habits in order to survive in the city.

e. _____ The shape of some animals' bodies has evolved as a result of their urban habitat.

C MAIN IDEAS Choose the main idea of the article.

a. Living in urban areas has caused genetic changes in several types of animals.

b. Urban animals are more successful than animals that live in the wild.

c. Human activity has led to evolutionary and behavioral changes in urban animals.

D DETAILS Complete the chart with the animals mentioned in the reading.

Animals that have changed their behavior while living in the city	Animals whose physical characterstics have evolved while living in cities

E DETAILS Check (✓) the six statements that you can infer from the article.

1. _____ Most animals thrive in an urban habitat.

2. _____ Cliffs and skyscrapers have similar characteristics.

3. _____ Urban animals are less likely than animals in the wild to be killed by predators.

4. _____ The behavior of the Japanese crows will probably spread to crows in other areas.

5. _____ Aggressive male juncos do not help with babies very much.

6. _____ Wing size varies more among wild swallows than among urban swallows.

7. _____ White-footed mice in New York eat a lot of food that people throw away.

8. _____ The adaptation of species to urban life is changing how scientists view evolution.

READING SKILL Distinguish counterarguments and refutations

To make an argument stronger, a writer can include possible objections to the argument in a **counterargument**. Acknowledging a counterargument shows that the writer has considered other sides of the issue and gives the writer the opportunity to respond with a **refutation**.

<u>Opponents insist that the project is far too expensive.</u> <u>The price tag is very high</u>, but
          counterargument   acknowledgement

<u>the investment will prevent costly problems in the future.</u>
          refutation

It's useful to distinguish between these ideas so that you are clear what a writer's opinion is. When you read, consider objections or counterarguments to the claims that the writer has made and how the writer responds to these objections in a refutation.

Counterarguments often begin with expressions such as:

Opponents believe . . .

Some people may object that . . .

One objection is . . .

An acknowledgement and refutation are often combined:

Although it's true that there are some problems with this idea, the benefits outweigh them.

F   APPLY Read the sentences. Identify and label the counterargument (C), the acknowledgement (A), and the refutation (R). Label them C, A, and R.

Opponents of the National Park City maintain that most other cities simply don't have enough green space to make the program worthwhile. Although it's true that the amount of park space in cities varies widely, even small steps toward preserving and expanding these spaces will lead to improvements in human health.

G   APPLY Reread paragraphs 1 and 5 of the article *Wild in the City*. Label the counterargument (C), the acknowledgement (A) if there is one, and the refutation (R).

REFLECT   Consider a claim about cities and nature.

Read the quote from psychologist and biologist Suzanne MacDonald. Then discuss the questions with a partner.

"We have this view of the wild as a pristine place [and of evolution as something that happens] in the wild. But humans in cities are changing the animals now. And with so many animals going urban, humans must view cities as part of—not separate from—nature."

1. What does MacDonald mean? Explain the quote in your own words.

2. What evidence, if any, does the article provide to support MacDonald's claim?

3. Do you think Daniel Raven-Ellison, the explorer in the video, would agree with this quote?

PREPARE TO READ

A VOCABULARY Read the sentences. Write the words in bold next to their definitions.

- ▸ Scientists **calculate** that wild birds outnumber humans 6 to 1.
- ▸ Chemicals from nearby factories can **contaminate** a city's water supply.
- ▸ One **critic** claims that small urban farms will not save a significant amount of resources.
- ▸ Farmers wait for the right time to **harvest** their fruits and vegetables.
- ▸ The UK has to **import** a large part of its food supply.
- ▸ Growing food at home is a nice hobby, but it's **impractical** as a way to feed a city.
- ▸ Today's farmers **integrate** modern technology into their farming practices.
- ▸ This idea has **potential**, but we need to work out the details for it to work.
- ▸ Mount Denali is very difficult to climb; in some places the rock is almost **vertical**.
- ▸ Modern farming has doubled the average **yield** per acre of wheat.

1. _____ (v) to bring in goods from another country
2. _____ (v) to make something dirty or less pure by adding something harmful
3. _____ (adj) at a 90-degree angle from the ground
4. _____ (adj) not sensible or easy to do
5. _____ (n) the amount that is produced
6. _____ (n) the ability to develop and succeed
7. _____ (n) a person who says they don't approve of something
8. _____ (v) to combine two things into one
9. _____ (v) to get a general idea about a cost or amount
10. _____ (v) to pick and collect crops (e.g., apples)

REFLECT Predict how to feed our cities.

Before you read an article about urban agriculture, study this information. Write answers to the questions in your notebook. Discuss your ideas with a partner.

1. How might city residents be affected by these statistics and trends?
2. What do you think are other ways to feed our cities?

Feeding the City

- The world has lost **30%** of its farmland since 1980.
- Today, **50%** of us live in cities; by 2050 it will be two thirds.
- **80%** of cities' food comes from rural farms.
- Many grapes that the British eat travel over **7,000 miles** (11,265 km) from Chile. Other foods travel similar distances.
- Over **2.6 million** trucks drive food to U.S. cities every day.

READ

FEEDING THE CITY

A APPLY Look at the photo and read the first paragraph. Answer the questions.

1. What do you think the article will be about?

2. What argument(s) do you think the writer will make to support this idea?

3. What counterargument(s) can you think of?

Vertical farming company Plenty, San Francisco, California, USA

1 In a huge warehouse in urban New Jersey, there's a new kind of farm and a new kind of farmer. Inside, from floor to ceiling, are rows and rows of lettuce plants. In a control room, staff use artificial intelligence to grow the perfect crop. Could farms like this one feed our growing city populations in the future?

2 While modern farms produce enormous quantities of food, it is still not enough to feed the whole planet. Ernst van den Ende, a Dutch agriculture scientist, **calculates** that we need to grow "more food in the next four decades than all farmers in history **have harvested** over the past 8,000 years." Producing more food using traditional methods may not be the solution to this problem. A typical farm uses a huge amount of resources, including land, water, and fossil fuels. It also uses fertilizers[1] and pesticides[2], sometimes **contaminating** the land and water nearby. Finally, because farms are generally far from cities, the food they produce has to travel long distances. As a result, the food is no longer very fresh when it arrives, and the whole process leaves a heavy carbon footprint[3].

3 What if food could be grown much closer to—or even inside—cities? Urban planners believe it will be essential in the future to **integrate** agriculture into our urban centers. In the last five years, this has started to happen—from the United States to Malaysia and the United Arab Emirates (UAE)—with the development of **vertical** farms. In these kinds of farms, plants are grown indoors in water filled with nutrients[4] instead of in soil, and they are planted vertically, not on the ground, as on a traditional farm.

4 These kinds of farms have several advantages over traditional farms. They can operate anywhere and in any season or climate. Because they are vertical, they use far less land, allowing them to operate in or near urban locations, where land is expensive. Vertical farms are extremely efficient; they have **yields** up to 350 times higher than traditional farms. One vertical farm company, Plenty, claims it can grow a million plants in a space the size of a basketball court. With vertical farms, cities that **import** most of their food, such as those located on islands or in deserts, can start producing some of their own. Finally, vertical farms are environmentally friendly. By recycling their water, they use about 70–90 percent less than traditional farms. And, since they are in a controlled environment, insects are not a threat, so there is no need for pesticides.

5 Not everyone is a big fan of vertical farming, however. **Critics** point to several drawbacks that make vertical farming **impractical**. First, vertical farming has been successful primarily with green leafy vegetables, such as lettuce, spinach, and herbs. It is a much bigger challenge to grow other vegetables and fruits. So, for now, the range of crops is limited. Second, and perhaps more important, this form of agriculture relies on electricity as a light source, which comes largely from non-renewable energy sources. This makes little sense, say critics, when the sun provides a free and renewable source of energy. Finally, it is very expensive to build and run vertical farms. Because of the high cost, this kind of agriculture may work for wealthy nations that lack farmland, such as Singapore or the UAE, but not for countries with fewer resources.

---

[1]**fertilizer** (n) a substance given to plants to help them grow

[2]**pesticide** (n) a chemical that kills harmful insects

[3]**carbon footprint** (n phr) the amount of carbon dioxide that an activity produces

[4]**nutrient** (n) a substance that living things need in order to grow

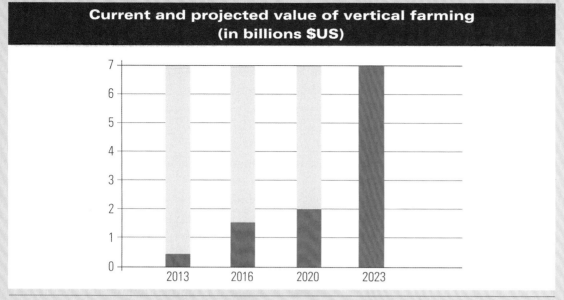

Current and projected value of vertical farming (in billions $US)

	7				
6					
5					
4					
3					
2					
1					
0	2013	2016	2020	2023

Figure 1

Source: BBC research

6   Supporters of vertical farming agree that this type of agriculture has limitations, but they believe it can make a significant contribution, particularly in cities. They argue that recent developments in the use of artificial intelligence have made vertical farms the perfect growing environment—even better than nature. Farmers can give each plant exactly the kind of light that it needs, exactly when it needs it. With the sun, they just have to accept what comes, but not every plant has the same light requirements. They argue further that costs are decreasing, especially the cost of the LED lights that are generally used in these facilities. With falling costs and improvements in technology, it may be possible to grow a wider range of crops in the near future.

7   Vertical farming is not going to meet all of the world's food needs, but it may help some cities give their populations fresher food with less impact on the environment. The business community is taking notice of its **potential**. The value of vertical farms has skyrocketed[5] in recent years (see Figure 1). The vertical farm company Plenty recently received major financial support from Japan's SoftBank, which runs the world's largest tech investment fund. The company plans to build vertical farms in every city with a population of 1 million or more. That's about 500 cities.

[5]**skyrocket** (v) to go up very quickly and suddenly

B MAIN IDEAS Choose five sentences that express the main ideas from the article.

  a. Some critics say that vertical farming isn't a realistic solution.

  b. Vertical farming provides 50 percent of the food for some major cities.

  c. We need to find new ways to feed growing cities.

  d. Traditional farming has several problems.

  e. Traditional and vertical farming use different light sources.

  f. Vertical farming offers some advantages over traditional farming.

  g. Food from vertical farms is more nutritious than food from traditional farms.

  h. Improved technology is making vertical farming a more practical option.

C DETAILS Read each statement. Write T for *True*, F for *False*, or NG for *Not Given* based on the information in the article.

1. _____ Pesticides used on traditional farms can poison nearby water.

2. _____ The plants in vertical farms grow in the air instead of in soil.

3. _____ Traditional farms can grow more kinds of crops than vertical farms.

4. _____ Urban indoor farms are more common in cold climates.

5. _____ Vertical farms use much less water than traditional farms.

6. _____ Vertical farms use solar energy, so they have a smaller carbon footprint.

7. _____ Artificial intelligence is used on traditional farms, too.

8. _____ Vertical farms use apps to deliver food to their customers.

D Complete the summary of the arguments, counterarguments, and refutations about vertical farms. Use the words in the box.

carbon footprint	energy	land	range
cost	environment	pesticides	yields

In the article, the author argues that vertical farming uses less ¹_____ and water than traditional farms. Vertical farms have higher ²_____ and do not need to use ³_____. In addition, vertical farms can be placed near cities, so food is fresher and there is a smaller ⁴_____. The author presents several possible counterarguments. One is that the ⁵_____ of crops that vertical farms can grow is fairly small. In addition, vertical farms use mostly non-renewable ⁶_____ rather than free sunlight. Finally, it's very expensive to operate vertical farms. The author refutes these objections by claiming that, in fact, vertical farms provide an ideal ⁷_____ for plants—better than nature. The author also says that the ⁸_____ of vertical farming is going down.

REFLECT Assess the impact of vertical farming.

Say whether you agree or disagree with each statement (1=strongly agree, 4=strongly disagree). Discuss your opinions in a small group.

1. Vertical farming is the answer to the planet's food crisis. **1 2 3 4**

2. Vertical farming could make a significant contribution in my community. **1 2 3 4**

3. Advances in technology and AI will make vertical farming more practical. **1 2 3 4**

Karl Johans Gate,
Oslo, Norway

WRITE

UNIT TASK Write a cause-effect essay about a change in a community.

You are going to write an essay in response to the question, "Think about a recent construction project or new policy in a city or community you know well. What were the reasons for this change, and what have been its effects?" Use the ideas, vocabulary, and skills from the unit.

A MODEL ESSAY Read the model essay. Then with a partner, discuss whether Oslo's restriction on cars has been successful.

How Restricting Cars Has Changed a City

1   Cars have transformed modern cities, and in many ways, they have made our lives easier. However, in many cities, commuters sit in long traffic jams, losing hours of productivity. In addition, cars are responsible for much of the world's pollution. Consequently, many cities have begun to question whether we really need all of these cars. By restricting the use of cars, cities like Oslo, Norway have significantly improved residents' health and well-being.

2   Oslo changed its policy on cars for several reasons. Oslo sits in a low area. As a result, air pollution often covers the city. This pollution can cause illness and shorten lives. City leaders were determined to decrease the level of pollution, which is primarily caused by gasoline-powered cars. They also wanted to encourage residents to walk and interact with each other in the center of the city. They thought that limiting cars would make the city more appealing for residents. For these reasons, Oslo banned cars on some streets. Then it improved and expanded public transportation and built bicycle paths. In 2019, the city removed more than 700 parking spaces, making it almost impossible to park in the city center.

3   These changes have greatly reduced pollution in Oslo. Car use in the city has dropped by nearly 10 percent in less than 10 years, contributing to a dramatic improvement in the city's air quality. In 2019, the city won the title of European Green Capital, in part for its efforts to limit the use of polluting vehicles. Oslo now has a goal of becoming a car-free and zero-carbon city by 2030.

4   The changes have also affected how Oslo residents go about their daily lives. More residents now take public transportation; others bike or just walk. Since the removal of the parking spaces, there has been a 10 percent increase in pedestrian traffic in the city center. City leaders believe this development is due to the reduction in vehicle traffic. Thanks to these changes, there are now parks and pedestrian-only streets. Approximately 1.3 km² of the city is car free, leaving these spaces open for social and cultural activities.

5   Opponents of the changes objected that without cars, businesses in the city would suffer. Some even said that the city center would be empty, yet this hasn't happened. Oslo's leaders maintain this success is the result of careful planning. While the changes were not easy to implement, even opponents agree that Oslo has become a much nicer place.

B ANALYZE THE MODEL Answer the questions.

1. What is the thesis statement?

_____

_____

2. What are the two main reasons Oslo restricted cars?

_____

_____

3. What have been the two main effects of Oslo's policy change?

_____

_____

4. What counterargument is introduced in paragraph 5? How is it refuted?

_____

_____

WRITING SKILL   Write about causes and effects

When you write about causes and effects, you can focus on 1) the causes or reasons something happened, 2) the effects or results of something, 3) both, or 4) a chain of causes/effects.

1. Focus on causes/reasons

Cause(s) ➜ [Event]

For example, an essay could explain three reasons to adopt vertical farming.

2. Focus on effects

[Event] ➜ Effect(s)

For example, an essay could describe the ways a city has been affected by the wildlife living in it.

3. Focus on causes and effects

Cause(s) ➜ [Event] ➜ Effect(s)

For example, an essay could explain several reasons to adopt vertical farming and describe the possible effects of that change.

4. Focus on a cause/effect chain

Cause ➜ Effect/Cause ➜ Effect

For example: *The lower cost of LED lights decreases the cost of vertical farming, which makes it more practical. As a result, vertical farms have become more common.*

C ANALYZE THE MODEL Check (✓) the approach the writer took in the model essay.

1. _____ focus on causes

2. _____ focus on effects

3. _____ focus on causes and effects

4. _____ focus on chain of effects

D APPLY Review the article *Wild in The City*. Complete the cause-and-effect chains. Use up to two words from the article for each answer.

a. Juncos live in the city. ➜ They have less ¹_____ lives there. ➜ They have bigger ²_____. ➜ Females choose less ³_____ males who help them find food for the babies.

b. Cliff swallows with long wings cannot turn quickly. ➜ ⁴_____ kill swallows that do not turn quickly. ➜ Only birds with ⁵_____ survive. ➜ The ⁶_____ for short wings spread through the ⁷_____.

c. White-footed mice live in small city ⁸_____. ➜ Their ⁹_____ are now very small. ➜ They don't have a wide choice of ¹⁰_____. ➜ Beneficial traits ¹¹_____ through the population quickly.

LEARNING TIP

Causes and **reasons** are similar, but they are not exactly the same. Causes generally refer to natural, physical, or historic processes, such as fires, accidents, diseases, or wars. Reasons often refer to processes and events that are under human control, such as decisions or behavior.

GRAMMAR Cause and effect connectors

The most common **cause and effect connectors** are *because* and *so*, but causes and effects can also be signaled with **prepositions** and **transitions**. Prepositions introduce causes (or reasons). They are followed by a noun phrase. Transitions introduce effects (or results). They are followed by an independent clause.

Because of _the tightly controlled growing conditions_, *vertical farmers don't use pesticides.*
preposition + cause   effect

Birds with shorter wings survived. **_As a result_**_, genes for short wings became more common._
      cause   transition + effect

Preposition + cause	Transition + effect
because of, due to, thanks to, as a result of, as a consequence of	as a result, consequently, therefore

E GRAMMAR Find the connectors in the model essay. Write the cause or effect that the connector introduces. Does it introduce a noun phrase or an independent clause?

1. Consequently, _____(paragraph 1)

2. As a result, _____(paragraph 2)

3. due to _____(paragraph 4)

4. Thanks to _____(paragraph 4)

F GRAMMAR Complete the sentences with a correct connector. More than one answer is possible.

1. _____ the efforts of Daniel Raven-Ellison, London is now a National Park City.

2. London was a good candidate for a National Park City _____ all of its green spaces.

3. City residents throw away a lot of food. _____, it's easy for urban animals to find enough to eat.

4. Evolution occurs _____ random genetic mutations.

5. Many animals are unable to cross busy roads. _____, animal populations in the city are generally smaller.

6. Evolution is speeding up _____ human activity.

G GRAMMAR In your notebook, rewrite these sentences using the cause and effect connector in parentheses.

1. Many people have left farms because there are new job opportunities in cities. (because of)

2. Many animals have left their wild homes because there is generally more food available in cities. (consequently)

3. Many urban animals have larger families than those that live in the wild because life is less stressful in the city. (as a result)

4. These mutations are helpful, so the animals can survive more easily in the city. (thanks to)

5. Transporting food from farms to cities uses a lot of energy, so it makes sense to move farms inside cities. (therefore)

6. Because their productivity is greater, modern farms can feed a lot more people than they could in the past. (because of)

7. It's difficult to grow large, heavy vegetables on vertical farms, so most of these farms grow smaller, lighter vegetables. (as a result)

8. The cost of this technology is quite high, so its use is not yet widespread. (due to)

H GRAMMAR For each topic, write sentences with connectors that introduce causes or effects. Use a preposition in one sentence and a transition in the other.

1. changes in animal behavior in urban areas

   a. _____

   _____

   b. _____

   _____

2. the use of fertilizer and pesticides

   a. _____

   _____

   b. _____

   _____

3. the restriction of cars in Oslo

   a. _____

   _____

   b. _____

   _____

PLAN & WRITE

I BRAINSTORM Answer the questions. Discuss your ideas in a small group.

1. What are some recent construction projects or policy changes in a city or community you know well? (You can also do some online research to find out about one.) Check (✓) the events or add your own ideas.

   ☐ building a new school   ☐ changing the road system

   ☐ tearing down an old factory   ☐ _____

   ☐ turning a park into apartments   ☐ _____

   ☐ building a new hospital   ☐ _____

2. Choose one project or change to write about. Make a list of the reasons why it's important. Talk to your family and neighbors or do research to find out more about it.

   _____

   _____

3. What have been the effects of the project on the community? Does it look different? Have people's lives changed? Are they better, worse, or different? Complete the chart.

Positive effects	Negative effects

City Lake beach in Almetyevsk, Tatarstan, Russia

J OUTLINE Complete the outline using your ideas from activity I. Decide if your essay will focus on reasons, effects, or both.

Introductory paragraph Hook: _____

Background information: _____

_____

General claim about the change: _____

_____

First body paragraph Reason or effect: _____

_____

Supporting ideas/Details: _____

_____

Second body paragraph Reason or effect: _____

_____

Supporting ideas/Details: _____

_____

Third body paragraph Reason or effect: _____

_____

Supporting ideas/Details: _____

_____

Concluding paragraph Final comment or prediction: _____

_____

K FIRST DRAFT Use your outline to write a first draft of your essay.

L REVISE Use this list as you write your second draft.

- ☐ Does your introduction catch the reader's attention?
- ☐ Does your thesis statement clearly express your claim about the change?
- ☐ Do your body paragraphs adequately describe the project itself, as well as the reasons for the project and/or its effects?
- ☐ Do your body paragraphs provide enough evidence to support your claim?
- ☐ Does your conclusion make a comment or prediction about the project?

M EDIT Use this list as you write your final draft.

- ☐ Did you use correct connectors to express causes and effects?
- ☐ Did you use the correct verb forms?
- ☐ Do your subjects and verbs agree?

N FINAL DRAFT Reread your essay and correct any errors. Then submit it to your teacher.

REFLECT

A Check (✓) the Reflect activities you can do and the academic skills you can use.

☐ consider how wild animals live in a city

☐ consider a claim about cities and nature

☐ predict how to feed our cities

☐ assess the impact of vertical farming

☐ write a cause-effect essay about a change in a community

☐ distinguish counterarguments and refutations

☐ write about causes and effects

☐ cause and effect connectors

☐ be an active reader

B Write the vocabulary words from the unit in the correct column. Add any other words that you learned. Circle words you still need to practice.

NOUN	VERB	ADJECTIVE	ADVERB & OTHER

C Reflect on the ideas in the unit as you answer these questions.

1. London is the first National Park City. What other cities do you think have the potential to become National Park Cities? Explain.

_____

_____

2. What is the most important thing you learned in this unit?

_____

_____

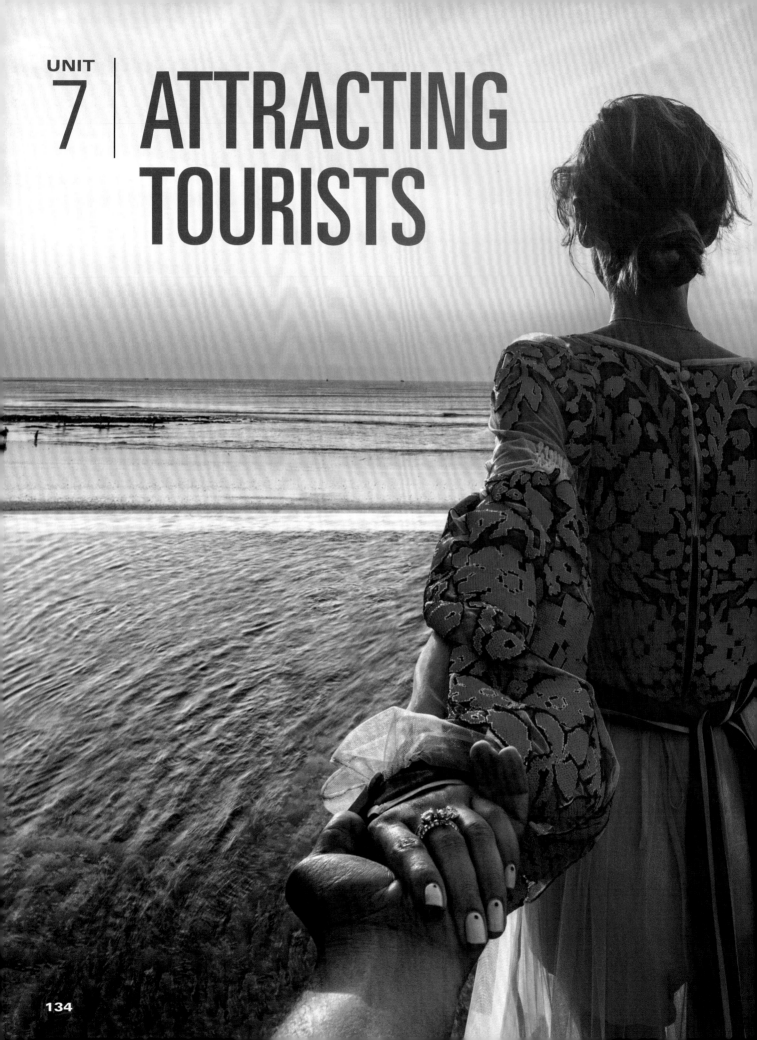

Jimbaran Bay, Bali, Indonesia

CONNECT TO THE TOPIC

1. Where are the people in the photo? Does the photo make you want to visit?

2. How do you decide where to go on vacation or on a trip?

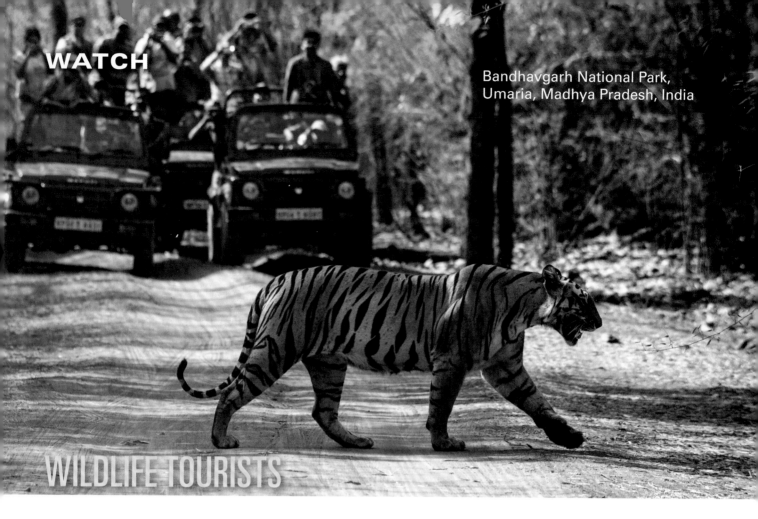

WATCH

Bandhavgarh National Park,
Umaria, Madhya Pradesh, India

WILDLIFE TOURISTS

A Watch the video. Check (✓) the two problems and two benefits of tourism mentioned. ▶7.1

Problems

1. _____ Too many tourists have put pressure on tigers.

2. _____ Some tourist vehicles have hit and killed tigers.

3. _____ Some tourists don't behave themselves because some guides aren't good.

Benefits

1. _____ Money from tourism can help wildlife such as tigers.

2. _____ Tourism increases people's connection to wildlife.

3. _____ Tourism attracts customers for local businesses.

B Watch the video again. Choose the correct word or phrase to complete each sentence. ▶7.1

1. Wildlife tourism in India makes **two to three / three to five / five to ten** million dollars a year.

2. Money from tourism goes toward **creating / protecting / planting** wildlife areas.

3. People in **rural / urban / poorer** areas are often not connected to nature.

4. **Taking photos / Playing sports / Walking into a forest** can bring people closer to nature.

5. Tigers have a fantastic **personality / history / appearance** that attracts thousands of tourists.

6. India's tigers raise public awareness around the **beauty / danger / conservation** of wildlife.

C PERSONALIZE Do you think the benefits of wildlife tourism outweigh the problems? Explain your answer in a small group.

PREPARE TO READ

A VOCABULARY Choose the correct meanings for the words in bold.

1. The explorer's blog gave a frightening **account** of the trip she took.

   The blog gave a **description / prediction**.

2. The hikers had waited for months and were **eager** to start the climb.

   They **really wanted to / were scared to** climb the mountain.

3. This city needs to invest more in their **infrastructure** to handle all the tourists.

   The **restaurants, shops, and entertainment / roads, bridges, and services** are not good enough.

4. Young people are usually more willing to take advice from their **peers**.

   They will take advice from **people who are similar to them / people who are more important than they are**.

5. The tourism office sends email messages to **potential** visitors around the world.

   The messages go to visitors **who are going to come / who might come**.

6. A closer look **revealed** that the photo had been edited to make the town look prettier.

   A closer look **hid / showed** how the photo had been changed.

7. The hotel manager offered a **sincere** apology for all the problems and gave them a large discount on their bill.

   The apology was **dishonest and fake / honest and real**.

8. City leaders are happy about the **steady** increase in tourists over the last 10 years.

   The increase has been **fast and sudden / smooth and constant**.

9. The photos of the animals that live around the coral reef were **stunning** and quite colorful.

   The pictures were **extremely beautiful / very frightening**.

10. This city is definitely **worthy of** a visit by anyone interested in architecture.

    I think it's **deserving of / possible to get** a visit.

REFLECT   Rank tourist attractions.

You are going to read a blog post about the impact of social media on tourism. Why do tourists visit your city or a city you know well? Rank the following factors (1 = most important to 6 = least important). Add one factor of your own. Then compare with a partner and explain your ranking.

_____ cafes and restaurants   _____ stunning scenery

_____ cultural experiences   _____ museums and galleries

_____ outdoor activities   _____ other: _____

AMAZING INFLUENCERS

A PREDICT Read the first paragraph of the blog post. What do you think happened after the influencers arrived? Discuss your ideas with a partner.

Photo of Lake Wānaka, Otago, New Zealand by Chris Burkard

1   Imagine a beautiful blue lake with world-class fishing, empty beaches, and **stunning** views. For many tourists, Lake Wānaka on the South Island of New Zealand sounds like the perfect vacation destination. Yet, not very many people knew about this place—until a group of social media influencers arrived.

2   For much of its recent history, Lake Wānaka's main industry was sheep farming. But, proud of Lake Wānaka's beauty, local leaders were **eager** to attract more tourists. Globally, the tourism industry contributes almost nine trillion dollars annually toward GDP[1]. That's more than 10 percent of the total GDP. For small communities like Lake Wānaka, tourism means a reliable income and jobs. Some jobs are directly related to the tourism industry, such as hotel and airport workers. Other jobs are indirectly related. For example, farmers and fishers supply the food that is served at hotels and restaurants where tourists stay and eat. Finally, tourism often contributes to **infrastructure**. Roads and airports may be built to bring tourists, but local residents benefit from them as well.

3   Because of the benefits tourism brings, it is a competitive business. Advertising is expensive—particularly for small places like Lake Wānaka. Until recently, most people learned about travel destinations by reading about them in guidebooks. That has all changed with the development of social media and in particular, Instagram. Instagram is one of the fastest-growing social media platforms, with one billion monthly users and half a billion active daily users. Users actively engage with the content, by liking, posting, clicking, and most important of all, buying. And for the tourism industry, that user engagement leads to travel decisions. Chris Burkard, a photographer with 3.5 million followers on Instagram, sums it up this way: "You're less than 10 clicks away from seeing an image on Instagram to purchasing a ticket to go there."

4   Lake Wānaka leaders hoped social media could increase tourism in their community at a lower cost than a traditional advertising campaign. So, they invited a group of travel influencers—including professional photographers—to Lake Wānaka. These influencers all had large numbers of followers online. The leaders wanted them to experience the region's beauty and activities. They also, of course, wanted the influencers to take photographs and post them with the hashtag #LoveWānaka. Chris Burkard was one of the people invited. His photos of the area got 50,000 likes almost immediately. The influencers' impact was remarkable. The area saw a 14 percent increase in tourist visits in 2016—the highest in the entire country that year. And it continues to draw a **steady** stream of visitors today. Local leaders have been thrilled with the results. The Lake Wānaka Tourism Board called it "an incredible return on investment[2]."

---

[1]**GDP** (n) gross domestic product—the value of everything produced in one year in a given country

[2]**return on investment** (n phr) the amount of profit compared to the amount invested

5   The impact of travel influencers has been enormous all over the world. They determine whether a location is **worthy of** Instagram, and therefore worth visiting. A recent survey of young travelers **revealed** that, for 40 percent of them, the most significant factor in their choice for a vacation destination was "Instagrammability." "I've met people who have traveled to places because of my photographs," says Burkard with some surprise. "That wasn't happening 10 years ago." Why do influencers have so much impact on the public's travel choices—even more than professional travel writers or advertisements? Travel professionals believe there are two main reasons. First, travelers view these influencers as **peers**, as people who are very much like them. They think: If these people liked this place, I probably will, too. Influencers' **accounts** seem more **sincere** than the reports of professionals. Second, and perhaps more important, Instagram is the perfect medium for visual storytelling.

6   Without a doubt, social media has helped Lake Wānaka, but it is not alone in benefiting from the impact of online platforms. Thirty years ago, Iceland got 142,000 visitors a year. In 2018, the island received more than two million. Much of that growth is the result of its highly "Instagrammable" landscape. Hoping to increase tourism, officials in Scottsdale, Arizona, recently hired artists to create wall murals. They chose popular areas for the paintings in order to create "Instagrammable moments." Some hotels have begun to redesign their lobbies to look attractive to **potential** guests on social media. Clearly, it has become a powerful tool that can help communities like yours attract tourists.

A mural in Scottsdale, Arizona, USA

B MAIN IDEAS Complete the summary of the blog. Use one word from the blog for each answer.

In many communities, tourism brings dependable [1]_____ and jobs. But tourism is competitive, and advertisements can be [2]_____. Social media [3]_____ like Instagram offer a cheap and effective way to raise awareness of a tourist destination. For example, travel [4]_____ with a lot of followers helped Lake Wānaka to attract tourists. Followers trust them because they think their stories are more [5]_____. Many communities are discovering that social media can be a great [6]_____ in their effort to increase tourism.

C DETAILS Read each statement. Write T for *True*, F for *False*, or NG for *Not Given* based on information in the blog.

1. _____ Before Instagram, Lake Wānaka didn't have a lot of tourists.

2. _____ The tourism industry is 10 percent of the GDP of New Zealand.

3. _____ Residents do not benefit from improvements in infrastructure.

4. _____ Tourism campaigns on social media are more expensive than traditional advertising.

5. _____ Instagram has a very high level of user engagement.

6. _____ Chris Burkard makes a lot of money from his online posts.

7. _____ The influencers' visit had a positive impact on tourism in Lake Wānaka.

8. _____ Social media has become an important element of the travel and tourism industry.

D DETAILS Check (✓) the three statements that you can infer based on information in the blog.

1. _____ Today, more people are probably working in the tourism industry in Lake Wānaka.

2. _____ Most small communities are using social media to increase tourism.

3. _____ For 60 percent of young people in the survey, "Instagrammability" was not important at all.

4. _____ It's likely that some people who saw Burkard's photos visited Lake Wānaka.

5. _____ Lake Wānaka now has too many tourists.

6. _____ Fewer people were using social media to make travel decisions 10 years ago.

READING SKILL   Recognize a writer's point of view

Point of view refers to a writer's opinion or perspective on a topic. As you read, look for the following.

1. Evaluative and descriptive words and phrases that imply the writer's opinion
   *There has been an **incredible** improvement.*
   *This is an **unfortunate** development.*

2. Adverbs and adverb phrases that express the writer's attitude toward a topic
   (e.g., *certainly, fortunately, in fact, of course, surely, unfortunately*)
   ***Indeed**, this is an effective strategy.* (*Indeed* emphasizes the point.)
   ***Sadly**, this has become a common practice.*

3. First and second person pronouns and possessive forms: These allow the writer to speak directly to the reader and help to include the reader in the writer's point of view.
   ***Your** community can easily increase the number of tourist visits.*
   ***We** can't let this happen to **our** community.*

Once you recognize the writer's point of view, you can decide if you agree with it or not.

E Choose the correct answers to complete the statements about the blog *Amazing Influencers*.

1. The writer has a **positive / negative** view about the value of tourism.

2. The writer has a **positive / negative** view about the value of social media.

F Answer the questions about the blog.

1. What three evaluative or descriptive words show the writer's point of view in paragraph 4? Highlight them.

2. What two adverbs or adverb phrases show the writer's point of view in paragraph 6? Highlight them.

3. How does the writer use a possessive form to include the reader in paragraph 6? Highlight the phrase.

REFLECT   Assess evidence in a travel blog.

Write answers to these questions in your notebook. Then discuss your ideas with a partner.

1. What evidence in the blog supports the writer's view that tourism in general is valuable?

2. What evidence supports the writer's view about the impact of social media on tourism in Lake Wānaka?

3. Has the writer convinced you that her point of view is right?

PREPARE TO READ

A VOCABULARY Choose the correct meanings for the words in bold.

1. Two monkeys were fighting in a tree, and I **captured** the whole thing on video.

   a. showed   b. posted   c. recorded

2. The movie was very violent, which many people in the audience found **distressing**.

   a. upsetting   b. surprising   c. extraordinary

3. We can feel **inferior** when we compare our lives to the lives of people on social media.

   a. happy for others   b. hopeful   c. not as good as others

4. Today, it's possible to **make a living** by teaching people how to cook online.

   a. find a job   b. earn enough money   c. live a long time

5. Sunlight can't easily **penetrate** thick gray clouds.

   a. cover   b. go through   c. warm up

6. In bad weather, hiking on the mountain trails is **prohibited**. It's too dangerous.

   a. not encouraged   b. not stopped   c. not allowed

7. We tried to **replicate** the vacation we had here years ago, but too much had changed.

   a. improve on   b. permanently record   c. do again in the same way

8. The wet summer **ruined** beach vacations for many people.

   a. destroyed   b. added to   c. changed

9. I got a great **shot** of my family standing in front of the Eiffel Tower.

   a. route   b. photo   c. view

10. My friend was **showing off** by telling everyone about her expensive jewelry.

    a. pretending not to care about   b. being mean about   c. attracting attention to

B PERSONALIZE Discuss these questions with a partner.

1. Do you think being an influencer is a good way to **make a living**?

2. Do you think posting on social media is **showing off**?

REFLECT   Consider pros and cons of tourism.

You are going to read a blog post about some of the effects of travel influencers. Work with a small group. Brainstorm ideas about the pros and cons of tourism in your community or a place you know well. Decide on the top two pros and cons.

Pros	Cons

IS SOCIAL MEDIA
HARMING TOURISM?

A PREDICT Read the title of the blog post and look at the photo and caption. What do you think the writer's purpose is?

Zhangjiajie Glass Bridge, Hunan, China

1   Let's face it, social media platforms have **penetrated** every aspect of travel, from how we choose a place to visit to what we do once we get there. Sadly, a few beautiful photos online can sometimes transform a quiet, remote corner of the world into a circus. In 2010, fewer than a thousand tourists visited Trolltunga, Norway, a spectacular rock formation 370 kilometers west of Oslo. Six years later, the number had climbed to 80,000. This increase followed the appearance of photos on social media. This process can happen extremely quickly. Amazing photos appeared online soon after the opening of a glass-bottom bridge over the Zhangjiajie Canyon in China. Within days, thousands of visitors arrived, all hoping to **capture** similar images. Because of the crowds, the government decided to temporarily close the bridge and **prohibit** people from visiting.

2   Clearly, social media provides the fuel for our vacation dreams, but it also has a negative side. Increasingly, travelers are choosing their vacation destination based on images they see online. They plan their vacations around the photographs they hope to post, already smiling about how their friends will react to them. Many travelers say they do this to share their wonderful experiences with their friends and family, but isn't this more like **showing off**? The **distressing** thing is that many of these tourists are not really looking at the natural beauty or exciting environment around them. Instead, they just want to take photos like the ones they saw online. Some travelers even hire professional photographers to follow them so they can get that perfect photo!

3   Some of these travelers are ordinary tourists, but others are trying to **make a living** as travel influencers. In an effort to attract more followers, these influencers find places that are more and more remote to take more and more spectacular pictures. These efforts may mean they go places where they should not or do things that are dangerous. In the old quarter of Hanoi, Vietnam, for example, visitors compete to take photos of themselves on the train tracks that run along the street. Some stand on the train tracks as long as possible, jumping off just as the train comes—so they can capture the most dramatic image.

4   Unfortunately, these influencers and tourists are not a danger just to themselves. Their activities can cause real damage to the locations that they are promoting. One recent newspaper article on this topic began, "Sorry Instagrammers. You are **ruining** Wyoming." Delta Lake is located in a remote area in the Wyoming mountains. Before social media, just a few visitors a day might find their way there. Today, the daily number is closer to 150, with some people making the 14.5-kilometer hike to take engagement or wedding photos. All of this traffic is damaging the environment and putting wildlife at risk. Local officials have asked visitors to stop geotagging[1] photographs on social media in order to protect the fragile ecosystem[2]. This distressing story is not limited to wild places. In 2018, a Canadian flower farm invited visitors to come admire their beautiful fields of flowers. The owners were unaware that word[3] was spreading through social media, and they were not prepared for the crowds. Shockingly, thousands of visitors arrived, climbing on ladders and destroying hundreds of flowers, hoping to get the perfect **shot**. The farmers closed their doors after about a week.

---

[1]**geotag** (v) to use electronic data to show where something is

[2]**ecosystem** (n) all the living things in an area

[3]**word** (n) news or information

A "superbloom" of flowers,
Lake Elsinore, California, USA

5 Everyone wants that perfect shot, and the photos on Instagram do look nearly perfect. Have you ever wondered why? Of course, many of the photos on Instagram are taken by honest, professional photographers, but many travel influencers edit their photographs to make the locations look better. They cut out the hundreds of tourists on a beach to make it seem as if there are no crowds, or they brighten the colors to hide air pollution. As a result, travelers are sometimes disappointed when they arrive at a destination and find it very different from the images they admired on social media.

6 Social media is a powerful tool, and we can use it to explore the world, but we need to use it thoughtfully. Travel writer James Asquith hopes that tourists stop relying so much on these "perfect" photos to make their travel choices and instead try to appreciate these locations as they really are. "It shouldn't all be about **replicating** what an 'influencer' has done. Pictures are important memories from our travels, but so are the experiences we have. Social media should genuinely inspire us to travel, rather than make our experiences seem **inferior** to what we have seen."

B MAIN IDEAS Put the main ideas in the order (1–6) that they appear in the article.

a. _____ Some Instagrammers are destroying the places they photograph.

b. _____ As they pursue more dramatic shots, some influencers are taking risks.

c. _____ Social media platforms are very effective for reaching and influencing tourists.

d. _____ We should try to enjoy real experiences and not depend on social media.

e. _____ Some travel influencers are dishonest.

f. _____ Some travelers spend so much time trying to take great photos that they don't really see what's around them.

C MAIN IDEAS What is the main purpose of the blog? Check (✓) the best answer.

1. _____ To explain the pros and cons of social media's impact on tourism

2. _____ To persuade us that social media can have a negative impact on tourism

3. _____ To describe ways that social media platforms could be better for tourism

D DETAILS Complete the sentences. Use the names of places or countries from the blog.

1. In _____, influencers risked their lives on railroad tracks.

2. In _____, a flower farm was destroyed by people trying to take photos.

3. In _____, 80,000 visitors a year began to arrive after photos were posted on Instagram.

4. In _____, hundreds of people hiked nine miles in a fragile ecosystem to take the perfect picture.

5. In _____, after photos appeared on social media, a bridge had to close due to crowds.

E Answer the questions about the blog.

1. What four evaluative or descriptive words show the writer's point of view in paragraph 4? Highlight them.

2. What two adverbs show the writer's point of view in paragraph 4? Highlight them.

CRITICAL THINKING Recognize bias

When a writer expresses a point of view but does not provide evidence to support it, this can be seen as **bias**. Bias means supporting (or opposing) a person or point of view based on personal preferences rather than facts. When you read a piece of argumentative writing, check to see how the writer's point of view is supported. You should be careful about accepting a writer's point of view if it's not supported by evidence.

REFLECT   Recognize bias in claims.

Read two claims that the writer of the blog makes about travel influencers. What evidence in the blog supports each claim? Is there enough evidence to support each claim or are they biased? Discuss your reasons in a small group.

1. Travel influencers often do stupid and dangerous things.

2. Travel influencers and the tourists they bring are damaging travel destinations.

WRITE

Oaxaca in southern Mexico is known for its artist communities.

UNIT TASK Write an argumentative essay about the impact of tourism.

You are going to write an argumentative essay in response to the question, "Has tourism had a positive or negative impact on your community or a community you know well?" Use the ideas, vocabulary, and skills from the unit.

A MODEL Read the model essay and decide what the writer's point of view is.

Is Tourism Beneficial for Oaxaca?

1   Oaxaca is one of the most beautiful states in Mexico, but it has not always had a lot of resources. Much of its economy has relied on agriculture and mining. This is hard, backbreaking work that does not always provide residents enough income. Today, though, the state's fastest-growing industry is tourism. Oaxaca's natural beauty and rich culture attract thousands of tourists from around the world. This change in the economy has been a positive development for the state.

2   Oaxaca has the greatest biodiversity of any state in Mexico. It has plants and animals found nowhere else. We have been able to protect this precious natural resource partly because many tourists want to experience nature. To respond to this demand for "eco-tourism," the government created huge nature reserves, especially along the coast. One example is Huatulco National Park, which protects thousands of species of animals. Some people complain that the tourists are disrespectful and behave badly. While that's true of some tourists, they are a minority.

Without tourists, we might not have this wonderful resource. Indeed, we might have factories there instead.

3   Nature is not the only attraction for tourists in Oaxaca. Our rich cultural heritage is also an important factor. The state is famous for its artistic traditions, including weaving, pottery, and woodcarving. These draw thousands of tourists to our state and promote valuable cultural exchange. The increase in tourism has brought some unwelcome changes; the price of housing has increased in the city center because of tourist hotels. However, most local people accept this. The artists know that the tourists provide them with a market for their work. Tourism also provides a steady income for people who act as guides.

4   It's really all about money—money that these tourists bring to our economy. Although some money goes to the central government, the government returns money to Oaxaca to help support infrastructure projects. The projects are aimed at increasing tourism. They include better roads and more reliable communication systems, especially, the Internet. Although tourism may be the reason for these projects, local residents also use and benefit from these services.

5   Tourism has generally improved the lives of people here and can continue to do so. We can use tourist dollars to help people who can no longer afford to live in the city center. We can be thoughtful and careful about how we develop the tourism industry here. Clearly, we need to control the number of tourists and their impact, but if we use tourism to make our lives better, we can continue to develop our community in harmony with nature and our traditions.

B ANALYZE THE MODEL Write the benefits the writer claims that tourism offers to Oaxaca. Then write the evidence the writer gives to support each benefit.

1. Paragraph 2
    Benefit: _____
    Evidence: _____
    _____

2. Paragraph 3
    Benefit: _____
    Evidence: _____
    _____

3. Paragraph 4
    Benefit: _____
    Evidence: _____
    _____

C ANALYZE THE MODEL Complete the examples of evaluative and descriptive language that the writer uses in the model essay.

1. a _____ development

2. a _____ resource

3. a _____ cultural exchange

4. _____ roads

5. more _____ communication systems

WRITING SKILL   Write counterarguments and refutations

When you write an argumentative essay, you use facts and evidence to convince your readers that your claim is valid. You can strengthen your essay by including **counterarguments**—objections a reader might have to your argument. You should **acknowledge** any counterarguments and then offer a **refutation**. The refutation states why the counterargument is not valid or correct.

Claim: Tourism is hurting our area.
Supporters of tourism maintain that tourism is the best way to improve the economy.
                             counterargument

These tourist dollars are indeed attractive. However, we have seen too many communities
        acknowledgment   refutation

suffer environmental and cultural harm as a result of tourism.

The counterargument and refutation are often connected by a contrast connector, such as *although, but, however, indeed, nevertheless, while, yet,* etc.

D ANALYZE THE MODEL Reread paragraphs 2 and 3 of the model essay. Identify the counterargument, the acknowledgment, and the refutation. Label them C, A, and R. Circle the word that connects the counterargument and the refutation.

E APPLY Match each refutation to the correct counterargument. Underline the acknowledgment. Circle the word that connects the counterargument and the refutation.

Counterargument

1. When it first appeared, Instagram was welcomed as a powerful tool to help communities attract tourists. And indeed, it was very successful, _____

2. Tourism is our primary source of income. It's true that we need tourists, _____

3. Supporters of the infrastructure projects argue that without them, tourists will choose to go somewhere else. Infrastructure is certainly important, _____

Refutation

a. but not if it replaces the natural spaces that are the reason that tourists choose our community as a destination.

b. but today it has become too successful and it is increasing tourism beyond the ability of communities to handle them.

c. yet we need to pay attention to the type of tourists we are trying to attract. We need more mature tourists who appreciate our culture and history.

F Complete the counterarguments with refutations. Use your own ideas.

1. In spite of claims that tourism has negative effects on local residents, _____

     _____ .

2. National park officials worry that hikers are destroying animal habitats, _____

     _____ .

3. Some people want to reduce the number of tourists worldwide. _____

     _____ .

GRAMMAR Articles

Nouns are introduced by the articles *a/an* or *the*—or with no article at all (Ø).
Follow these steps to help you choose the correct article.

1. First, decide if you can use **the**. Use *the* if you think your readers will know the specific thing, person, place, or idea you are mentioning. Readers will know if:
    - ▸ you already mentioned it with either the same word or a synonym.
      I took a trip to Oaxaca. **The** *experience was amazing.*
    - ▸ you share knowledge of it: **the** *government,* **the** *moon,* **the** *store,* **the** *graph below.*
    - ▸ it is part of, or connected with, something you have already mentioned:
      I left <u>my car</u> at home, but I think I left **the** *windows open.*
    - ▸ it is unique or part of a ranking: **the** *only, one of* **the** *X,* **the** *second,* **the** *best.*

2. If *the* is not appropriate, you can use:
    - ▸ **a/an** for count nouns.
    - ▸ no article (Ø) for noncount and plural nouns.
      I want to save Ø money for **a** *trip to Indonesia.*

G GRAMMAR Look at paragraph 2 of the model. Why does the writer use *the*? Write the reasons (a–d).

a. The writer already mentioned it with either the same word or a synonym.
b. The writer and you share knowledge of it.
c. It is part of, or connected with, something that the writer has already mentioned.
d. It is unique or part of a ranking.

1. _____ the greatest biodiversity

2. _____ the government

3. _____ the coast

4. _____ the tourists are disrespectful

H GRAMMAR Complete the paragraph with *the* or *a* or *an*. Discuss the reasons for your choices with a partner.

¹_____ increasingly popular form of tourism is medical tourism, that is, people crossing international borders for medical care. ²_____ medical tourism market is estimated to be over 50 billion dollars per year. ³_____ most popular destinations are India, Malaysia, Singapore, and Thailand. Why would people travel for ⁴_____ medical procedure? ⁵_____ most important factor is cost. This is especially true for American patients, who can save up to 90 percent, compared to their health-care costs at home. India has seen ⁶_____ steady rise in medical tourism, so ⁷_____ country is trying to make it easier for tourists to come. In 2015, ⁸_____ Indian medical tourism market was worth about 3 billion dollars; by 2020, ⁹_____ figure had jumped 200 percent.

I EDIT Read the paragraph. Find and correct eight errors with *the*, *a*, or *an*.

There is the museum in Turkey for people who like to visit strange sites. The museum displays local pottery, but it also has the collection of hair. There is an old story that a woman who lived in this town wanted to leave the friend with something that would help him remember her. So, she gave him the piece of her hair. The man hung the hair up in his pottery shop and told the story to his visitors. The women who visited his shop loved a story, so they left him pieces of their own hair. Soon a man had so many pieces of hair that he turned his shop into a museum. Inside the museum, there is the pair of scissors so that visitors can add a piece of their own hair to a collection.

Avanos, Nevşehir, Turkey

PLAN & WRITE

J BRAINSTORM Follow these steps.

1. Think about a city or place you know well where there is a lot of tourism. Write the name.

   _____

2. How does tourism impact the place you chose? Discuss these areas of impact with a partner. Add one idea of your own.

   What is the impact on . . . ?

   ▸ jobs

   ▸ income for local shops and artists

   ▸ traffic and pollution

   ▸ police and health professionals

   ▸ infrastructure projects

   ▸ natural spaces

   ▸ culture

   ▸ shops and restaurants

   ▸ prices for food and other necessities

   ▸ opportunities for young people

   ▸ rents and home prices

   ▸ _____

3. Complete the chart. Choose three areas of impact that you think are most important for the place you chose. Write down arguments for and against tourism. Add evidence to support each argument.

Area of impact	Arguments for tourism	Arguments against tourism

K OUTLINE Complete the outline using two of the areas of impact from activity J.

Introduction

Background information: _____

Claim about the impact of tourism: _____

Thesis statement: _____

_____

First body paragraph

Area of impact: _____

Evidence: _____

_____

Counterargument: _____

Acknowledgment: _____

Refutation: _____

Second body paragraph

Area of impact: _____

Evidence: _____

_____

Counterargument: _____

Acknowledgment: _____

Refutation: _____

Conclusion _____

_____

L FIRST DRAFT Use your outline to write a first draft of your essay.

M REVISE Use this list as you write your second draft.

☐ Do you provide enough background information?

☐ Does your thesis statement clearly express your claim about the impact of tourism?

☐ Do your body paragraphs provide enough evidence to support your point of view?

☐ Do your body paragraphs present, acknowledge, and refute a counterargument?

☐ Does your conclusion make a comment or prediction about tourism in the community you are writing about?

N EDIT Use this list as you write your final draft.

☐ Did you use persuasive language appropriately?

☐ Did you use articles correctly?

☐ Did you use the correct verb forms?

O FINAL DRAFT Reread your essay and correct any errors. Then submit it to your teacher.

REFLECT

A Check (✓) the Reflect activities you can do and the academic skills you can use.

- ☐ rank tourist attractions
- ☐ assess evidence in a travel blog
- ☐ consider pros and cons of tourism
- ☐ recognize bias in claims
- ☐ write an argumentative essay about the impact of tourism

- ☐ recognize a writer's point of view
- ☐ write counterarguments and refutations
- ☐ articles
- ☐ recognize bias

B Write the vocabulary words from the unit in the correct column. Add any other words that you learned. Circle words you still need to practice.

NOUN	VERB	ADJECTIVE	ADVERB & OTHER

C Reflect on the ideas in the unit as you answer these questions.

1. Now that you have learned more about tourism, do you think it has an overall positive or negative impact? Why do you think so?

2. Did anything in this unit change how you will use social media for travel and tourism? How?

3. What is the most important thing you learned in this unit?

UNIT
8
BREAKING RECORDS

American skier Lindsey Vonn competes in Cortina d'Ampezzo, Italy.

IN THIS UNIT

▶ Consider the role of genes in athletic performance

▶ Analyze a quote about sports

▶ Consider the impact of technology on sports

▶ Predict the future of sports records

▶ Write an opinion essay for a standardized test

SKILLS

READING
Skim and scan during a standardized test

WRITING
Write an essay for a standardized test

GRAMMAR
Combine modals

CRITICAL THINKING
Synthesize information from different sources

CONNECT TO THE TOPIC

1. Look at the photo. What kind of challenges do you think athletes like Lindsey Vonn face?

2. Who do you think is the greatest athlete in history?

157

WATCH

HOW FAST CAN WE RUN A MARATHON?

The Moscow Marathon, Russia

A PREDICT You are going to watch a video about running a marathon—a 26-mile (42-kilometer) race. How fast do you think humans can run a marathon? Watch the video and check your prediction. ▶ 8.1

B Watch an excerpt from the video. Write T for *True* or F for *False* for each statement. ▶ 8.2

1. _____ The marathon has its origin in ancient Greece.

2. _____ Running is less popular than many other sports.

3. _____ Participation in marathons has grown almost 50 percent.

4. _____ A runner completed the marathon in less than two hours for the first time in 2010.

C The video mentions that marathon runners can improve three physiological processes in their bodies. Watch an excerpt from the video. Match the elements to the ways that athletes can improve them. One choice is extra. ▶ 8.3

Marathon runners can improve their . . .

1. oxygen consumption by _____

2. lactate threshold by _____

3. running efficiency by _____

a. building strength through resistance training.

b. finding a better running technique.

c. drinking more water.

d. training at high altitudes.

PREPARE TO READ

A VOCABULARY Read the sentences. Write the words in bold next to their definitions.

▸ When you use your muscles, your cells **absorb** sugar from the blood, which gives you energy.

▸ This is a **crucial** decision, so we need to take the time to consider all our options.

▸ The **distribution** of the population across many countries is uneven. More people live in cities than in rural areas.

▸ Every four years, the World Cup **dominates** the sports news. Other sports barely get mentioned.

▸ Due to its length, many people say a marathon is the greatest test of an athlete's **endurance**.

▸ Sales of celebrity-sponsored shoes have been **explosive**. Everyone is buying them.

▸ In the summer, temperatures reach their **peak** in the afternoon before cooling down later.

▸ A retail company will collect useful data to create a customer **profile**.

▸ Strong wind **resistance** will slow down a runner or biker.

▸ A goal of the International Olympic Committee is to **stimulate** interest in athletics.

1. _____ (v) to encourage growth or development
2. _____ (adj) having sudden and great force
3. _____ (v) to take in
4. _____ (n) a description of someone's characteristics
5. _____ (v) to be the most important or to control
6. _____ (n) the highest point
7. _____ (n) a force that stops something or slows it down
8. _____ (n) the way things or people are spread out in an area
9. _____ (adj) extremely important
10. _____ (n) the ability to do something difficult or painful for a long time

REFLECT Consider the role of genes in athletic performance.

You are going to read about how genes affect athletes' performance. Study the pie chart. Then answer the questions in a small group.

1. Which group of respondents do you agree with? Explain.

2. What aspects of athletic success do you think are most influenced by genes? Consider these areas: coordination, endurance, flexibility, skill, speed, and strength.

How much do you think athletes' genes contribute to their success?

None (28%)

A lot or almost all (39%)

Some or very litte (33%)

Source: Survey of 1200 randomly chosen people in the United States, University of Michigan

BORN TO **WIN**

Kalenjin athletes
training in Iten, Kenya

READING SKILL I Skim during a standardized test

Skimming means reading quickly to get a general understanding of the topic, the main ideas, and the claims the writer is making. Skimming is especially useful when you are taking a standardized test because your time is very limited. To skim efficiently, first read the title and subheads, if there are any. Then read the first, second, and last sentences of each paragraph. It's better to skim *before* you read the test questions to get a general idea of the content. This will make it easier to understand the questions and answer them.

A APPLY Skim the article. Then choose the main idea of the article.

    a. Athletes will continue to break records.

    b. Scientists are helping athletes to improve their performance.

    c. Genetics plays a major role in athletic success.

8.1

1 Between 2001 and 2009, swimmer Michael Phelps broke 39 world records across a range of events—including the 200-meter butterfly[1] world record eight times. He has won far more medals than any other athlete in Olympic history. His astonishing achievements seemed unbeatable. Yet, 10 years later, Hungarian swimmer Kristóf Milák beat the 200-meter butterfly record by 0.78 seconds. In fact, only four of Phelps's world records still stand today. Can athletes continue to break world records like this?

2 A study in 2008 suggested that major improvements in athletic performance were behind us. After reviewing 40,000 races from 1896 to 2008, Geoffroy Berthelot, one of the authors of the study, claimed that athletic performance hit its **peak** in 1988. Yet, more than 30 years after that date, records of speed, strength, and **endurance**, including Phelps's, continue to be broken. Clearly, humans keep getting better. And although training, hard work, and motivation are all important, the source of their success is often beyond the control of even the greatest athletes. Instead, it mainly results from the many genes that control how their bodies are shaped and behave.

3 We are all born with different body shapes, and specific body shapes and sizes are ideally suited to different sports. For example, the ideal body shape for swimming is in the shape of a triangle, with big shoulders, a long torso[2] and narrow hips. Phelps was born with this body shape and improved it with training. His shoulders and long arms, which measure 80 inches (203 centimeters) across from fingertip to fingertip, give him enormous power. His narrow hips at the bottom of the triangle result in less **resistance** as he moves through the water, and his legs, which are shorter than average, give him a powerful kick. Other sports require different body types. For example, long-distance runners are typically very light and have long, thin legs but short torsos, like the Kalenjin people of Kenya. Their body type has evolved over a long history to help them stay cool in a hot, dry climate. Today, that also helps them **dominate** long-distance running. Kenyans are relatively recent competitors in global athletics, which may explain why they continue to break records today.

---

[1]**butterfly** (n) a type of swimming style

[2]**torso** (n) the part of the human body without arms, legs, or head

4   Body shape is just one part of how athletes' bodies contribute to their success. Different sports make specific demands on the muscles. Some, such as 100-meter events in swimming and running, require short, intense effort. Others, like the marathon, require endurance. There are two types of muscle fibers[3]. *Slow-twitch muscle fibers* contract— or become shorter—more slowly and can work for long periods of time without tiring. In contrast, *fast-twitch muscle fibers* contract more quickly and are stronger, but they run out of energy faster. Everyone is born with a different **distribution** of these muscle fibers. Athletes with a higher percentage of fast-twitch muscle fibers are better suited to sports such as sprinting[4], diving, and weightlifting, which require quick, **explosive** energy. Those with more slow-twitch muscle fibers are more likely to succeed in sports that require endurance. Athletes can strengthen all their muscles through training, but they cannot change the distribution of muscle fibers they were born with.

5   Another **crucial** factor in athletic success is how the body uses oxygen. VO_2 max is a measure that shows how much oxygen your body can **absorb** and use. The greater the VO_2 max, the more oxygen the body can use to generate the maximum amount of energy. It is the key to success in many sports, especially cycling, which depends on lung power. Athletes can increase their VO_2 max and therefore, their performance, through training. However, here, too, genes can play a role. Oxygen is carried by red blood cells, and the production of red blood cells is **stimulated** by a chemical called EPO. Some people have a naturally stronger response to EPO because of a genetic mutation[5]. Finnish skier Eero Mäntyranta had this genetic mutation, which allowed his body to produce 25–50 percent more red blood cells than average. As a result, Mäntyranta's muscles got more oxygen, so he could ski faster and longer, winning two gold medals in the 1964 Olympics.

6   Scientists are beginning to understand the role of these and other genetic factors in athletic performance. Most agree that their role is crucial, and in some cases, perhaps more important than how hard an athlete works. Genetic analysis can reveal which athletes are best suited to which sports, as well as what type of training and diet will help them improve their performance. This allows coaches to identify which athletes have the greatest potential. It is possible that future champions—and future records—will be the result of identifying athletes with the perfect genetic **profile**.

---

[3]**fiber** (n) a long, thin material that forms a type of tissue in the body

[4]**sprinting** (n) running very fast for a short distance

[5]**mutation** (n) a change that makes something different from normal

Michael Phelps competes in the men's 100 meter butterfly.

B MAIN IDEAS Write the paragraph number (2–6) next to the correct heading.
Two headings are extra.

a. _____ Oxygen Use During Exercise

b. _____ The Importance of Body Shape

c. _____ The Role of Age in Athletic Success

d. _____ The Future Role of Genetics in Sports

e. _____ The Ideal Sport for Your Height and Weight

f. _____ Can Records Still Be Broken?

g. _____ Matching Muscle Fiber Types to Sports

READING SKILL II   Scan during a standardized test

Scanning means finding specific details in an article. Scanning for details such as names, numbers, and dates can help you quickly answer test questions. During a test, follow these steps to scan effectively:

▸ First, read the questions and identify key words (dates, names, terms, places).
▸ Then scan the text and look for those key words. Pay attention to numbers, capital letters, and words in italics.
▸ When you have found the information you are looking for, skim the nearby sentences to make sure you understand the context.
▸ When you are scanning for a key word, keep in mind that the question may use a synonym.

C APPLY Read each statement. Identify a key word that will help you scan for more information about each statement. Use the key word to scan for information in the article. Then, for each statement, write T for *True*, F for *False*, or NG for *Not Given*.

1. _____ Recent sporting events prove that the 2008 study was wrong in some respects.

2. _____ Michael Phelps has broad shoulders.

3. _____ Kalenjin runners have the ideal body shape for sprinting.

4. _____ Kenyan runner Eliud Kipchoge is one of the most successful long-distance runners.

5. _____ Humans generally have more fast-twitch muscle fibers than slow-twitch muscle fibers.

6. _____ Energy generation is the key to athletic success.

7. _____ Mäntyranta succeeded because he took illegal drugs.

8. _____ Genetic profiles may predict future record breakers.

D DETAILS Complete the information about how genes improve athletic performance. Use one or two words from the article for each answer.

Body shape

1. The best body type for swimming is in the shape of a _____.

2. Phelps's shape means less _____ as he swims.

3. _____ runners often have long legs.

Muscles

4. _____ muscle fibers can work for a long time without getting tired.

5. _____ muscle fibers get tired faster.

6. People with more _____ muscle fibers are better at sports that need sudden bursts of energy.

Oxygen absorption

7. The ability to absorb oxygen is important for sports that need _____ power.

8. Because of a genetic _____, some people have a better response to EPO.

REFLECT Analyze a quote about sports.

Read the quote. Write answers to the questions in your notebook. Then discuss your ideas in a small group.

"Sport has the power to change the world. It has the power to inspire, it has the power to unite people in a way that little else does. . . . Sport can create hope, where once there was only despair."

—Nelson Mandela, former president of South Africa

1. Do you agree that sports have the power to change the world? Explain.
2. What are examples of sporting events that have created hope or united us?
3. What are some benefits of sports that go beyond physical health?

Cricket fans cheer for their team in Brisbane, Australia.

PREPARE TO READ

A VOCABULARY Match each word with its definition. Use a dictionary if necessary.

1. _____ apparel (n)
2. _____ bounce (v)
3. _____ dimensions (n)
4. _____ drain (v)
5. _____ elite (adj)
6. _____ frontier (n)
7. _____ have to do with (v phr)
8. _____ indicator (n)
9. _____ momentum (n)
10. _____ monitor (v)

a. measurements
b. a signal or sign
c. best; most skilled
d. the border between what is known and what is unknown
e. the force that keeps an object moving
f. to watch a situation carefully
g. clothing; things to wear
h. to be about; to be related to
i. to reduce; to take away
j. to move up or away after hitting a surface

B Complete the paragraphs with words from activity A.

a. Most ¹_____ basketball players are very tall. As a result, they sometimes have trouble finding ²_____ that fits the ³_____ of their bodies.

b. Clothing companies ⁴_____ social media influencers to assess the latest trends. Increased interest in a brand or style of sportswear is a(n) ⁵_____ that they should make more of these clothes.

c. Technology is the next ⁶_____ in athletics. For example, new types of running surfaces are helping runners to increase their ⁷_____.

REFLECT Consider the impact of technology on sports.

Before you read an article about the impact of technology on sports, think about how athletes have gotten stronger and faster. How much do you think the following advances in technology have contributed to this trend? Discuss your ideas with a partner.

▸ New designs and materials for sports apparel
▸ More advanced equipment
▸ Smart devices that monitor performance
▸ Scientifically designed training programs
▸ Video analysis of performance
▸ Other: _____

HOW FAST CAN WE GO?

Victor Campenaerts riding the bike designed for him, Ghent, Belgium

A PREVIEW Skim the article. Choose the best alternative title.

a. New Frontiers in Athletic Training

b. A Technology Revolution in Sports

c. The Future of Sports Is Now

8.2

1 In 1936, Jesse Owens broke the world record for the 100-meter race, in 10.2 seconds. Seventy-three years later, Usain Bolt became the fastest man in the world, with a time of 9.58 seconds for the same distance. The difference between Owens's and Bolt's records seems small, but 0.62 seconds is huge in such a short race. How did Bolt go so much faster than Owens? One reason is the track. Owens ran on a cinder[1] track, which **drains** energy from runners' legs, whereas Bolt ran on a smooth rubber track, which returned energy to his legs as they **bounced** off it. Bolt also got a faster start by pushing off from starter blocks. Bolt, like all modern athletes, has benefited from innovations in equipment, **apparel**, and training that have allowed him to go faster than ever before.

2 High-tech equipment is taking seconds off records, particularly in cycling. **Elite** cyclists are constantly looking for new bike designs to give them an advantage. In 2019, Victor Campenaerts set a new world record for the longest distance cycled in one hour. His bicycle was an amazing technological achievement, with a frame and seat designed to fit the exact **dimensions** of his body. It was almost as if his body and his bicycle were one single unit. This gave him an aerodynamic[2] shape, reducing wind resistance and helping him cycle faster. This change in design made a dramatic difference. Campenaerts's record was over five miles farther than the record set in 1972 by Eddy Merckx. In contrast, when other 21st-century cyclists attempted to outdo Merckx's record using a bike similar to the one he originally used, they were able to beat his record by only 883 feet (270 meters).

3 Changes in athletic apparel are also helping swimmers and runners go faster. Consider swimwear, which for women, once included skirts and belts. Today's swimwear **has** little **to do with** fashion. Instead, these tight swimsuits compress[3] the swimmers' muscles, which helps athletes recover after competition. The swimsuits are made of fabric that is modeled on the skin of sharks, engineered to reduce resistance and help swimmers move smoothly through the water. When these suits were introduced in the 2008 Olympics, swimmers broke 25 world records, which is the highest number since the introduction of the last major advance in swimwear—goggles[4]. Recent improvements in athletic shoes have helped runners to achieve record-breaking performances. In 2020, Kibiwott Kandie broke the record for the half-marathon by 29 seconds. He was wearing lightweight shoes which are specially designed to give each step **momentum**, allowing him to run faster but with the same amount of energy.

[1]**cinder** (n) a small piece of partly burned wood

[2]**aerodynamic** (adj) having a shape which reduces the resistance from air moving past

[3]**compress** (v) to press something into a smaller space

[4]**goggles** (n) special glasses for swimming or protecting the eyes

4   What's the next **frontier** in athletic apparel? Smart clothing that uses sensors[5] to tell athletes what is going on in their bodies is the latest development. These sensors can **monitor** heart rate, breathing, and how much oxygen is in the blood, all **indicators** of how much energy the athlete is using. These sensors may also be able to help long-distance runners cope with one of their greatest challenges: staying hydrated. If athletes don't drink enough, they cannot give their maximum effort, but if they drink too much, they may begin to feel heavy or even sick. One product currently in development is a wearable sensor that tells athletes when and how much they need to drink.

5   Training has also gone high-tech, with many professional athletes starting to use virtual reality (VR) for both physical and mental training. Coaches are hoping this technology will help their athletes build speed and skill. VR has become part of the training program for Olympic skiers. In the VR environment, they can practice going down a course over and over again, without the danger of falling and risking injury. Troy Taylor, a director on the U.S. ski team, says, "The clear advantage of VR is that it is a great way to help athletes get more used to and learn specific courses." When the skiers get to the real course, their performance is smooth and automatic, and Taylor hopes, faster.

6   Technology will never replace talent or hard work. However, today, when elite athletes break records by just centimeters or fractions of a second, a little help from technology can make a big difference.

---

[5]**sensor** (n) a small device that can detect changes

B MAIN IDEAS Check (✓) the four statements that summarize the main ideas. The other statements either summarize less important points or describe ideas the writer does not mention.

1. _____ Technology advances have dramatically enhanced the performance of modern athletes.

2. _____ Fifty years ago, few athletes paid much attention to their shoes or clothes, but breakthroughs in apparel have shaved seconds and even minutes off record times.

3. _____ Mental training has become more important than physical training, and here, too, technology is playing an important role.

4. _____ Aerodynamic equipment and clothing cut down on air and water resistance.

5. _____ Technological innovations in training are improving performance and reducing injuries.

6. _____ Modern, high-tech equipment is helping athletes, from runners to cyclists, go faster.

7. _____ No one knows how many records will be broken in the future.

C DETAILS Identify one key word in each statement to use for scanning. Then complete the sentences with one or two words or numbers from the reading.

1. Staying hydrated is a problem for _____ runners.

2. Special shoes may have helped Kibiwott Kandie break a record for the _____.

3. Skiers are using _____ to visualize their races.

4. _____ broke the 100-meter record without the advantages of today's athletes.

5. Perfecting an aerodynamic shape is important for _____.

6. In 2009, Bolt beat Owens's record by _____.

D DETAILS Read each statement and scan the article for the information. Write T for *True*, F for *False*, or NG for *Not Given*.

1. _____ Modern methods of measuring time have led to faster race times.

2. _____ Modern swimwear uses fabric that is similar to bird feathers.

3. _____ Campenaerts' bicycle design helped him break a record by reducing wind resistance.

4. _____ It can be difficult for runners to decide how much to drink before or during a race.

5. _____ Women's swimsuits once had long sleeves.

6. _____ Virtual reality can help skiers avoid getting hurt.

CRITICAL THINKING   Synthesize information from different sources

When you read about different aspects of a topic from several sources, it's important to consider the ideas together. Do the sources agree, contrast, or provide additional details? For example, one source may say that we are at the limit of what a human body can do, whereas another may claim that technology can improve athletic performance even further. From this you might conclude:

▸ This issue is not settled. More research needs to be done.
▸ One source may be more reliable than the other. I should find out more about the sources.

REFLECT   Predict the future of sports records.

Consider what you have learned from the two articles. Check (✓) the three factors you think will improve athletic performance the most. Then discuss your ideas with a partner.

_____ better training methods
_____ better equipment
_____ more high-tech apparel
_____ specialized diets and medicines

_____ more realistic virtual reality simulators
_____ more accurate matching of genetic
profiles to specific sports
_____ Other: _____

WRITE

Opening ceremony of the Olympic
Games in Rio de Janeiro, Brazil, 2016

UNIT TASK   Write an opinion essay for a standardized test.

You are going to write an essay in response to the test question, "Do you agree or
disagree with the following statement? Anyone can become a successful musician,
artist, or athlete with enough hard work and training." Use the ideas, vocabulary, and
skills from the unit.

A MODEL Read the model essay for the question, "Some athletes have genetic
mutations that give them an advantage. Do you think these athletes should be allowed to
participate in the Olympics?" Then with a partner, decide what the writer's opinion is and
whether you agree with it.

Who Should Be Allowed to Compete in the Olympics?

1   Sporting events like the Olympics are celebrations of cooperation as well as
competition. They are a time for the best athletes to come together. All athletes must be
permitted to compete in the Olympics because genetic differences do not clearly provide
benefits and can't be controlled by an individual athlete.

2   It is true that scientists have discovered some genetic differences that help certain athletes, but it is unlikely that all of these differences have been discovered. Others may be discovered in the future. If we exclude athletes who have known genetic mutations, there may still be athletes with unknown mutations that help them perform better. Genetic mutations are common, so there are probably hundreds or thousands of genetic differences among athletes. This has probably been true since athletic competition began, and it will continue to be true into the future. One mutation may be an advantage, whereas another one may be a disadvantage. It is impossible to decide who should and who should not compete based on genetics. It would be unfair to choose one mutation for exclusion.

3   Another more important reason that these athletes should be allowed to compete is that these genetic mutations are natural. They are part of these athletes' bodies, just like the color of their skin and the length of their arms. Are we going to say that people who are taller than seven feet should not be able to play in basketball games, or people with really long arms will not be allowed to take part in swimming events? Athletes cannot control their genes, so it would be unfair to blame athletes for how they affect their bodies.

4   International athletics bring joy to people all over the world. Of course, competition should be fair, and everyone can agree that athletes who use drugs to change their bodies will need to be banned from competition. However, we must accept the natural genetic diversity of the human body and allow all athletes to compete in the Olympics.

B ANALYZE THE MODEL Answer the questions.

1. What is the writer's thesis statement? Underline it.
2. What are the main reasons the writer offers as support for the claim in the thesis statement?

    a. Paragraph 2: _____

    _____

    b. Paragraph 3: _____

    _____

3. What is the writer's conclusion? Underline it.

WRITING SKILL   Write an essay for a standardized test

Many standardized tests ask you to give your opinion on a topic in a 250–300 word essay. Because most tests are only 30 or 40 minutes, you must manage your time effectively to do well. For example, in a 40-minute test, you could:

- ▸ read the question carefully and check how many words you need to write (1 minute)
- ▸ brainstorm ideas and plan your essay (5 minutes)
- ▸ write your essay (30 minutes)
- ▸ check and correct your essay (4 minutes)

Follow these steps:

1. Include a short introductory paragraph, at least two body paragraphs that develop one main idea, and a concluding paragraph.

2. Paraphrase—don't copy—the test question in your thesis statement. Rephrase your thesis statement in the concluding paragraph.

3. Briefly acknowledge and refute possible counterarguments.

4. Vary your vocabulary and use synonyms instead of repeating words.

5. Use complex sentences—sentences with dependent clauses.

C ANALYZE THE MODEL Answer the questions.

1. Look at the test question. In the model essay, highlight the synonyms the writer uses in the thesis statement for these underlined words.

    "Some athletes have <u>genetic mutations</u> that <u>give them an advantage</u>. Do you think these athletes should be <u>allowed</u> to <u>participate in</u> the Olympics?"

2. How does the writer acknowledge any counterarguments? Underline the acknowledgments.

3. Look at these words. What synonyms or words with similar meanings does the writer use in paragraph 2?

    a. genetic mutation _____

    b. not include _____

    c. participate _____

4. Compare the concluding paragraph in the model essay to this alternative version. Which paragraph do you think would get a higher score? Explain your answer.

    International athletics bring joy to people all over the world. Of course, competition should be fair. Everyone can agree on one thing. We must ban athletes who use drugs. However, we must accept and celebrate the natural diversity of the human body. We must allow all athletes to compete to the best of their ability.

D APPLY Read each test question. Decide what your opinion is. Then write a thesis statement in response to each question in your notebook.

1. Employees are not productive when they work from home: They just waste their time. Do you agree or disagree?

2. We are putting too much stress on children by pushing them to learn academic skills in school when they are very young. Do you think it is better for children to just play in their early years?

3. People will not do things for the public good, such as using seat belts or wearing masks when they are sick, unless they are required by law. Do you agree or disagree?

WRITING TIP

Your essay will be judged on how clearly you develop your argument and how accurately you use the language, *not* on the content of your ideas. So, you should not spend a lot of time trying to think of arguments that are particularly original or even interesting.

E APPLY Choose one of the thesis statements you wrote for activity D. Write it in the center of the mind map. For three minutes, brainstorm ideas for an essay. Then add reasons or facts that support your thesis statement.

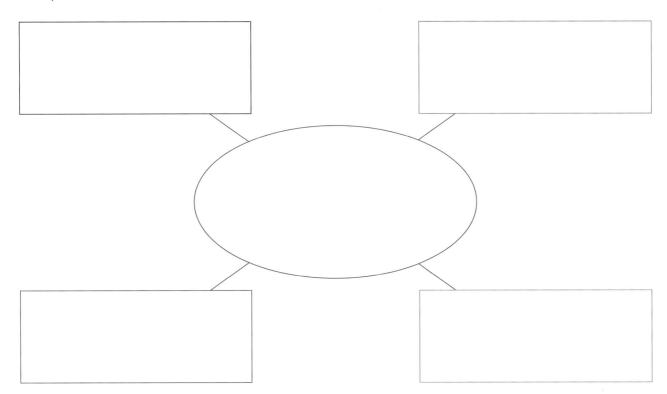

F APPLY Choose two of your supporting ideas from activity E. Add a few details for each of them to your mind map. Spend no more than three minutes.

G APPLY Read the test question and skim the essay. Then complete the essay with your own ideas.

"Do you agree or disagree with the following statement? Employees are less productive when they work from home than when they work in an office."

Why Working from Home Doesn't Work

These days more and more people want to work from home. They argue that working from home saves them time and helps them have a better balance with their personal lives. However, in my opinion, workers who work remotely get less done than those in an office because ¹_____ and ²_____.

When employees work at home, there are many distractions. Maybe they have a family. Their children often want their attention. They want to play. They want a snack. They need help with their homework. However, even if workers are alone, there are distractions such as ³_____. It is very easy to stop working. It is easy to do something more fun.

Another disadvantage is that there is no pressure to work. Employees don't like it, but it's clear that pressure is an effective way to push them. If an employee's boss is in the next office, that employee will ⁴_____. In addition, employees compete with each other in an office to show that they are more productive. If an employee never sees what other employees are doing, that employee doesn't feel that pressure. It is too easy to become lazy and stop working hard at home.

Although some people enjoy working at home because ⁵_____, it is not a good long-term policy. In order to have an efficient and productive office, it is important for employees to come into the office, where ⁶_____.

H Review the first body paragraph in activity G. In your notebook, rewrite the paragraph using more complex sentences.

I Review the second body paragraph in activity G. What word do you think is repeated too often? In your notebook, rewrite the paragraph using more vocabulary variety.

GRAMMAR Combine modals

Modals and phrasal modals are used to make suggestions, recommendations, and predictions, and to describe ability. You can combine modals and phrasal modals to express more complex ideas and to add variety to your writing.

A phrasal modal can be combined with a modal verb. The modal verb always comes first.

> All athletes **will need to** arrive by 5:00.

> NOT: All athletes ~~need to will~~ arrive by 5:00.

Some phrasal modals can follow another phrasal modal. The most common phrasal modals in these combined expressions are *be going to* and *have to.*

> All participants **are going to have to** finish the race in less than four hours.

> Athletes **have to be able to** pay their own expenses.

A modal verb cannot be combined with another modal verb.

> NOT: All athletes ~~will must~~ arrive by 5:00.

J GRAMMAR Reread the model essay in activity A. Underline four examples of modal combinations in the model.

K GRAMMAR Complete the sentences with the correct form of a phrasal modal in the box. Some questions have more than one correct answer.

be able to	be allowed to	be going to	be supposed to	have to	need to

1. No one will _____ use the gym after 5:00. It's being cleaned at that time.

2. The races didn't go very well, so we _____ need to schedule a meeting about future training.

3. We are supposed to _____ use the pool on weekends, but the door is locked.

4. If the weather is good, she should _____ finish the race in less than 45 minutes.

5. I _____ need to ask everyone to wait outside until the athletes have arrived.

6. He used to _____ run a four-minute mile, but he's slower now that he is older.

7. All the children _____ be allowed to take home a souvenir, but they will _____ wait until the game is over.

8. The athletes _____ be allowed to warm up before they start the race.

L EDIT Read the paragraph. Find and correct five errors in the use of modals and phrasal modals. Use a modal + a phrasal modal in your correction.

Slowing Down

When I was young, I used to can run 10 miles with no problem at all. Now, it's difficult for me to run more than two miles without my knees hurting. Now that I'm retired, I know that I'm supposed to could relax and enjoy life, but I really miss running long distances. I think I'm going to must try out a different exercise plan that is a little less stressful. I think I still might could do something such as biking or swimming—an activity where I don't use my knees so much. I have to talk to my doctor, and I think I'll must do it soon. My knees are killing me.

PLAN & WRITE

M BRAINSTORM AND PLAN Read the test question. Decide your opinion and brainstorm for five minutes. Use a mind map and take notes in your notebook.

"Anyone can become a successful musician, artist, or athlete with enough hard work and training. Agree or disagree."

N DRAFT Use your notes to write your essay. Time yourself. You should spend no more than 30 minutes.

> ### WRITING TIP
>
> When you take a standardized writing test, you won't have time to write a second draft of your essay. You can, however, spend a few minutes making minor revisions and correcting any errors.

O EDIT Use this list to check your essay. Take no more than three minutes. Then submit it to your teacher.

- ☐ Does your thesis statement clearly express your opinion?
- ☐ Is the language of the thesis statement different from the statement in the test question?
- ☐ Do each of your body paragraphs clearly express one reason?
- ☐ Do your body paragraphs provide enough evidence to support your reasons?
- ☐ Does your conclusion repeat your thesis in a new way?
- ☐ Did you use modals and phrasal modals correctly?

REFLECT

A Check (✓) the Reflect activities you can do and the academic skills you can use.

- ☐ consider the role of genes in athletic performance
- ☐ analyze a quote about sports
- ☐ consider the impact of technology on sports
- ☐ predict the future of sports records
- ☐ write an opinion essay for a standardized test

- ☐ skim and scan during a standardized test
- ☐ write an essay for a standardized test
- ☐ combine modals
- ☐ synthesize information from different sources

B Write the vocabulary words from the unit in the correct column. Add any other words that you learned. Circle words you still need to practice.

NOUN	VERB	ADJECTIVE	ADVERB & OTHER

C Reflect on the ideas in the unit as you answer these questions.

1. Who is your favorite athlete? What factors do you think are responsible for the athlete's success?

   _____

   _____

2. What is the most important thing you learned in this unit?

   _____

   _____

Formal and informal language

In professional or academic settings—such as in a report or an essay—you are likely to use more formal language. In casual or more personal settings—such as an email or a text to a friend—you often use less formal language.

More formal: She **regretted** her mistake.
multi-syllable word

More informal: She **was sorry about** her mistake.
multi-word phrase

In formal language, you often use more multi-syllable, single words. In informal language, you often use shorter words and multi-word phrases.

A Match the informal language with the more formal language. Check your answers in a dictionary.

More informal

1. _____ suggestion

2. _____ people

3. _____ home

4. _____ join in

5. _____ far away

6. _____ a little

More Formal

a. habitat

b. participate

c. remote

d. humanity

e. implication

f. slightly

B Replace the informal words in bold with the formal words from the box. One word is extra.

assemble	combine	demonstrate	exclusively	research	trigger	unique

1. The results of the study **show** that images can improve your memory of a written text.

2. The marketing people told special customers this offer was **only** for them.

3. Students can **look up** farming and agriculture to learn about where food comes from.

4. In the first step of the research study, children have to **put together** a puzzle.

5. The expedition to the Galapagos was a **once in a lifetime** experience.

6. Some classes **mix together** students from several different grade levels.

Phrasal verbs with *turn* and *wear*

A phrasal verb is a two- or three-word phrase. It always contains a verb and one other small word called a particle. The meaning of some phrasal verbs is easy to guess.

    I got up *early this morning.* = to rise from a chair or bed

The meaning of other phrasal verbs is less obvious. In addition, many phrasal verbs have multiple meanings.

    I like to **make up** *stories.* = to create or invent

    I'm glad we **made up**. = to become friends again after a fight

Use the context to guess the meaning of a phrasal verb first. Then look up the definition in a dictionary.

A Choose the best meaning of the phrasal verbs in bold. Check your answers in a dictionary.

1. I **turned down** the job offer because the salary was too low.

    a. to make quieter   b. to refuse   c. to fold

2. After a long, hard day studying, I was **worn out**.

    a. to become tired   b. to become damaged   c. to become weak

3. When I need advice, I **turn to** my grandmother.

    a. to move your face towards   b. to become involved with   c. to go to for help

4. When everything goes wrong, it seems like the whole world **turns against** you.

    a. to stop supporting   b. to use in order to harm   c. to move away from

5. Her long-lost earrings finally **turned up** under the sofa.

    a. to point upward   b. to appear   c. to arrive at a place

B Answer the questions about yourself.

1. When was the last time you felt **worn out**? _____

2. What is something you often **wear out** and need to replace? _____

3. Who was the last person you **turned to** for advice? _____

4. What was the last offer you **turned down**? _____

5. Think of something you once lost. Where did it **turn up**? _____

Prefixes *pre-* and *re-*

Remember: A prefix comes at the beginning of some words. The prefix *pre-* means "before" and the prefix *re-* means "again" or "backwards." When you see a new word beginning with these prefixes, you have a clue to help you understand the meaning.

> *I need to **prepare** for the test.* = to get something ready beforehand
>
> *We cannot **reverse** the aging process.* = to go back to an earlier state

The prefixes *pre-* and *re-* can also be added to words to make new words.

> *I **prepaid** my hotel bill.* = to pay for something before getting it
>
> *I will **repay** you for your help.* = to do or give something in return

A Complete each definition with the correct form of a word from the box. Two words are extra. Check your answers in a dictionary.

precede	predict	prepare	preserve	prevent	relocate	revert

1. When you guess what you will read before reading a text, you _____ the content.

2. When you go back to a former state, you _____ to it.

3. When you stop something before it happens, you _____ it.

4. When you move to a new place, you _____.

5. When an event happens before another event, it _____ it.

B Add *pre-* or *re-* to each word to make a new word. Then write a definition. Check your answers in a dictionary. More than one answer is possible.

1. _____ view: _____

2. _____ think: _____

3. _____ test: _____

4. _____ plan: _____

5. _____ act: _____

6. _____ heat: _____

Base words and word roots

A base word is a word that can't be broken into smaller words. You can often add affixes— suffixes or prefixes—to a base word to make it into a word with a different meaning or form.

cycle	***recycle***	***cyclist***
base word	prefix + base word	base word + suffix

Some base words are built from Greek or Latin roots. Knowing the meaning of word roots can help you understand unfamiliar vocabulary.

The word root *cycl* comes from Greek and means "circle".

A Add an affix to each base word to make a new word. More than one answer is possible. Use a dictionary to help you.

Prefixes		**Suffixes**			
in-	un-	-er	-or	-ion	-ly

1. fair _____

2. contribute _____

3. secure _____

4. supply _____

5. current _____

6. invest _____

B Review the definitions of these words from Unit 4. Then choose the best meanings of the word roots in bold.

1. _____ con**tribute**   a. limit

2. _____ dis**rupt**ed   b. give

3. _____ sup**port**ive   c. break

4. _____ de**term**ined   d. carry

C Complete the sentences with the words from the box. One word is extra. Use your knowledge of the word roots to help.

at**tribute**d	e**rupt**ed	ex**port**ed	**term**inated

1. After the volcano _____, everything was destroyed.

2. The business _____ most of its products overseas.

3. She _____ her success to hard work and luck.

4. Because of his poor performance, his contract was _____.

Suffixes *-able* and *-ible*

Remember: A suffix comes at the end of some words. The suffixes *-able* and *-ible* mean "able to."

You can add *-able* and *-ible* to some verbs to change them to adjectives. If the verb ends in *-e*, drop the *-e*. If the verb ends in *-y*, change the *-y* to an *-i*.

Adjective	Verb
My brother is very **likable**.	Everyone <u>likes</u> my brother.
The damage isn't **reversible**.	You can't <u>reverse</u> the damage.

There are also many adjectives ending in *-ible* that are not formed from verbs.

*The movie was **incredible**.*

A Write the correct adjective form of the words using either *-able* or *-ible*. Use a dictionary to help you.

Verb	Adjective		Verb	Adjective
1. flex	_____	5.	access	_____
2. sustain	_____	6.	value	_____
3. rely	_____	7.	distinguish	_____
4. break	_____			

B Complete the adjective with *-able* or *-ible*. Use a dictionary to help you.

1. Some people think that wearing shorts in the winter isn't **sens** _____.

2. Advances in technology made the Internet **poss** _____.

3. Precious stones like diamonds and rubies are not very **afford** _____.

4. Most apps are **compat** _____ with different models of smartphones.

5. Solar and wind power are examples of **renew** _____ energy solutions.

6. At the moment, it isn't **feas** _____ for humans to live on Mars.

7. Atoms are **invis** _____ to the human eye.

8. These plants are all **adapt** _____ to cold climates.

C Four adjectives from activity B are formed from verbs. Write the verb.

_____ _____ _____ _____

Prefixes *il-, im-, ir-, in-,* and *un-*

The prefixes *il-, im-, ir-, in-,* and *un-* mean "not." You can add these prefixes to some adjectives to give them the opposite meaning.

*If something is **im**possible, it means that it is not possible.*

Follow these rules:

▶ Use *il-* with adjectives that start with *l*: *illiteracy*

▶ Use *im-* with adjectives that begin with *p, m,* and *b*: *impossible*

▶ Use *ir-* with adjectives that begin with *r*: *irrelevant*

Most other adjectives use *in-* or *un-*, such as *inadequate* or *unable*. However, there is no easy way to know which of these prefixes to choose. If you are not sure, check the spelling in a dictionary.

A Write the opposite of the words. Use the prefixes *il-, im-, ir-, in-,* and *un-* .

1. secure _____

2. practical _____

3. wise _____

4. logical _____

5. significant _____

6. formal _____

7. fair _____

8. regular _____

9. legal _____

10. pleasant _____

11. moral _____

12. rational _____

B Complete the sentences with words from activity A. More than one answer may be possible.

1. In my country, driving a car before you are 15 is _____.

2. It is _____ to believe that things can change on their own.

3. Some people think that having too much money is _____.

4. When someone feels sad, they might be feeling _____.

5. When I talk to my friends, I often use _____ language.

Polysemy Multiple-meaning words

Polysemy refers to a word that has two or more different meanings. Sometimes the meanings are similar but not exactly the same. To understand which meaning is being used:

▶ Determine which part of speech the word is.

▶ Use context clues to help you understand the meaning of the word.

▶ Check the meaning of the word in a dictionary.

For example:

*His glasses showed a **reflection** of the clouds in the sky.*

You can tell from the placement of the word and its form that *reflection* is a noun. A dictionary says that *reflection* means: **1** an image repeated on a shiny surface, **2** a shining, and **3** a careful thought. In this example, then, *reflection* must be the first definition: the glasses are showing an image of the clouds.

A Choose the best meaning for the words in bold. Check your answers in a dictionary.

1. At the trial, the defendant gave his **account** of the accident.

    a. money kept in a bank
    b. a description
    c. to explain

2. The singer only **shot** to fame late last year but is now a household name.

    a. to hit or throw
    b. a photograph
    c. to move or happen quickly

3. That photo really **captures** the beautiful beach we vacationed at last year.

    a. to take someone by force
    b. to hold the attention of
    c. to show in an accurate way

4. The **key** issue facing the world today is climate change.

    a. most important
    b. a part of a machine that is pressed
    c. a written explanation

5. The **bond** between a mother and her child is very strong.

    a. a relationship of trust
    b. to stick together
    c. a certificate of debt

6. One of the most effective ways to get a job is to **network**.

    a. a system of connected routes
    b. to connect several computers together
    c. to connect with people in one's profession

7. I've been lucky to have a **steady** group of friends my whole life. They're always there to help when I need it.

    a. not shaking or moving
    b. dependable or reliable
    c. happening slowly and smoothly

Suffixes *-ant / -ent* and *-ance / -ence*

The suffixes *-ant / -ent* can be added to some verbs to make nouns or adjectives. They often mean "someone that does" (noun) or "doing a certain thing or being a certain way" (adjective).

An **assistant**'s job is to <u>assist</u> others.
noun

If something is heat **resistant**, it <u>resists</u> heat.
adjective

The suffixes *-ance / -ence* can also be added to some verbs to make nouns. They often mean "quality, action, or state."

An <u>assistant</u> is someone who gives **assistance** to others.
noun

Generally, you will need to learn and remember the spelling for these words. If you are not sure, check the spelling in a dictionary.

hesitate → hesit**ant**   urge → urg**ent**

accept → accept**ance**   exist → exist**ence**

A Write the correct form of the words in parentheses using *-ant / -ent* or *-ance / -ence*. Use a dictionary to help you.

1. She works for a financial company as a _____ (consult).

2. The political leader of many countries is a _____ (preside).

3. A cloth that can collect a lot of water is _____ (absorb).

4. If you keep working on a difficult problem until you get it right, you are _____ (persist).

5. Marathon runners must have a lot of _____ (endure).

6. An athlete who wins all the time is _____ (dominate) in their sport.

B Complete the chart. Check your answers in a dictionary.

Verb	Noun (with -ant or -ent)	Adjective (with -ant or -ent)	Noun (with -ance or -ence)
1. attend			
2. correspond			
3. persist			
4. rely			
5. reside			
6. resist			
7. tolerate			

VOCABULARY INDEX

*Academic words

VOCABULARY INDEX

TIPS FOR READING FLUENTLY

Reading slowly, one word at a time, makes it difficult to get an overall sense of the meaning of a text. As a result, reading becomes more challenging. In general, it is a good idea to first skim a text for the gist, and then read it again more closely so that you can focus on the most relevant details. Use these strategies to improve your reading speed:

- ▶ Use section headings, as well as the first and last lines of paragraphs, to help you understand how the text is organized.
- ▶ Read groups of words rather than individual words.
- ▶ Keep your eyes moving forward. Read through to the end of each sentence or paragraph instead of going back to reread words or phrases.
- ▶ Use clues in the text—such as bold words and words in italics—to help you know which parts might be important and worth focusing on.
- ▶ Skip structure words (articles, prepositions, etc.) and focus on words and phrases carrying meaning—the content words.
- ▶ Use context clues, affixes, and parts of speech—instead of a dictionary—to guess the meaning of unfamiliar words and phrases.

TIPS FOR READING CRITICALLY

As you read, ask yourself questions about what the writer is saying. Think about why the writer is presenting the information in the text. Important critical thinking skills for academic reading include:

- ▶ **Analyzing**: Examining a text closely to identify key points, similarities, and differences.
- ▶ **Applying**: Deciding how ideas or information might be relevant in different contexts, e.g., applying possible solutions to problems.
- ▶ **Evaluating**: Using evidence to decide how relevant, important, or useful something is. This often involves looking at reasons for and against something.
- ▶ **Inferring**: "Reading between the lines," in other words, identifying what a writer is saying indirectly rather than directly.
- ▶ **Synthesizing**: Gathering appropriate information and ideas from more than one source and making a judgment, summary, or conclusion based on the evidence.
- ▶ **Personalizing/Reflecting**: Relating ideas and information in a text to your own experience and viewpoints.

TIPS FOR NOTE-TAKING

Taking notes will help you better understand the overall meaning and organization of a text. Note-taking also enables you to record the most important information for future uses, such as when you are preparing for an exam or completing a writing assignment. Use these techniques to make your note-taking more effective:

▶ As you read, underline or highlight important information such as dates, names, and places.

▶ Take notes in the margin. Note the main idea and supporting details next to each paragraph. Also, note your own ideas or questions about the paragraph.

▶ On a separate piece of paper, write notes about the key points of the text in your own words. Include short headings, key words, page numbers, and quotations.

▶ Use a graphic organizer to summarize a text, particularly if it follows a pattern such as cause-effect, compare/contrast, or chronological sequence.

▶ Keep your notes brief by using abbreviations and symbols like these.

approx. approximately	**& / +** and	**>** is more than
➔ leads to / causes	**Ch.** Chapter	**<** is less than
e.g. / ex. example	**b/c** because	**~** is approximately / about
↑ increases / increased	**p.** page; **pp.** pages	
↓ decreases / decreased	**w/** with	**info** information
i.e. that is / in other words	**re:** regarding, concerning	**yrs.** years
	w/o without	**para.** paragraph
etc. and others / and the rest	**incl.** including	**excl.** excluding
	= is the same as	∴ therefore

TIPS FOR ACADEMIC WRITING

There are many types of academic writing (descriptive, argumentative/persuasive, cause-effect, etc.), but most types share similar characteristics. Generally, in academic writing, you should:

▶ write in full sentences.

▶ use formal English. (Avoid slang or conversational expressions such as *kind of*.)

▶ be clear and coherent—keep to your main point; avoid technical words that the reader may not know.

▶ use connecting words or phrases and conjunctions to connect your ideas.

▶ have a clear point (main idea) for each paragraph.

▶ use a neutral point of view—avoid overuse of personal pronouns (*I, we, you*) and subjective language such as *nice* or *terrible*.

▶ use facts, examples, and expert opinions to support your argument.

▶ avoid using abbreviations or language used in texting. (Use *that is* rather than i.e., and *in my opinion*, not *IMO*.)

▶ avoid starting sentences with *or, and,* or *but*.

CONNECTING WORDS & PHRASES

To give an opinion	To give examples	To link ideas/to add information
In my opinion, . . . I (generally) agree that . . . I think/feel (that) . . . I believe (that) . . . It is my personal view that . . .	An example of this is . . . Specifically, . . . For instance, . . .	Furthermore, . . . Moreover, . . . In addition, . . . Additionally, . . .
To present similar ideas	**To present different/contrasting ideas**	**To give reasons**
Similarly, . . . Both . . . and . . . Like . . . , . . . Likewise, . . .	However, . . . On the other hand, . . . In contrast, . . . Conversely, . . . Despite the fact that . . . Even though . . . Unlike . . . , . . .	This is because (of) . . . This is due to . . . One reason (for this) is . . . This is a consequence of . . . For this reason, . . .
To show results or effects	**To describe a sequence**	**To conclude**
Therefore, . . . As a result, . . . Because of this, . . . If . . . , then . . .	First (of all), . . . Then/Next/After that, . . . As soon as . . . Once . . . Finally, . . .	In conclusion, . . . In summary, . . . To conclude, . . . To summarize, . . .
To summarize/paraphrase	**To analyze and critique a text**	**To explain a concept**
Overall, the text argues that . . . The main point is . . . The author feels that . . .	The significance of . . . is . . . This is a good/poor example of. . . This is important because . . . This is a strong/weak argument because . . .	This is like . . . Think of this as . . . Essentially, this means . . . In other words, . . .
To refer to sources	**To give evidence or present facts**	**To convey attitude**
According to . . . , In the article . . . , . . . asserts/argues/claims/states . . . We know from . . . that . . .	There is evidence/proof . . . Studies show . . . Researchers found . . . . . . tells us/shows us/proves that . . .	Certainly, . . . Clearly, . . . Of course, . . . Sadly, . . . Surely, . . . (Un)Fortunately, . . .

Reflect is designed to provide practice for standardized exams, such as IELTS and TOEFL. This book has many activities that focus on and practice skills and question types that are needed for test success.

READING • Key Skills	IELTS	TOEFL	Page(s)
Read or skim for main ideas	x	x	9, 14, 31, 37, 52, 57, 75, 80, 97, 102, 119, 124, 141, 146, 147, 161, 163, 168
Read or scan for specific details	x	x	9, 10, 15, 31, 37, 53, 57, 75, 81, 97, 102, 103, 119, 125, 141, 147, 163, 164, 169
Predict what you will read	x	x	6, 12, 50, 56, 73, 78, 94, 100, 138, 144
Understand charts and graphs	x		15, 28, 76, 77, 78, 102
Make inferences	x	x	9, 53, 54, 119, 141
Preview a text	x	x	28, 34, 116, 166
Recognize points of view or bias	x	x	142, 147
Reading skills for tests	x	x	161, 163
Recognize counterarguments and refutations	x	x	120, 150
Understand pronoun references		x	98, 103
Read actively	x	x	122
Synthesize information	x	x	169
Recognize coherence and cohesion	x	x	81

READING • Common Question Types	IELTS	TOEFL	Page(s)
Multiple response	x	x	18, 38, 52, 54, 58, 61, 119, 124, 141, 168
Complete sentences, a paragraph, or a summary	x		15, 58, 75, 125, 141, 147, 164, 169
Match information to categories		x	15, 37, 40, 76, 97, 98, 103, 105
Match main ideas to paragraphs	x		9, 14, 31, 80, 97, 102, 119, 163
Judge if details are true, false, or not given	x		53, 75, 97, 125, 141, 163, 169
Match information to a paragraph	x		10, 17, 53, 81, 107
Multiple choice	x	x	75, 119, 147, 161
Complete a table, a chart, a diagram, or some notes	x		9, 31, 119, 128
Put information in order		x	37, 146

WRITING • Key Skills	IELTS	TOEFL	Page(s)
Brainstorm ideas	x	x	21, 43, 65, 86, 131, 153, 173, 176
Plan or outline what you will write	x	x	22, 44, 66, 88, 109, 132, 154
Review and edit to fix errors or improve	x	x	20, 42, 43, 64, 86, 152, 176
Write an essay	x	x	18, 22, 44, 66, 88, 132, 154
Analyze graphs, charts, or other visuals	x		28, 76, 77, 121, 159
Write a test essay	x	x	172, 173, 174, 176
Describe a graph, chart, or other visual	x		18, 76, 77, 121
Refute arguments	x	x	150, 151
Write about causes and effects	x	x	128, 130
Write counterarguments and refutations	x	x	150, 151
Organize an essay	x	x	18, 39
Write a paragraph	x	x	18, 42
Use hedging language	x	x	62, 66
Paraphrase	x	x	84, 85
Summarize information	x	x	106

WRITING • Common Topics	IELTS	TOEFL	Page(s)
Travel and tourism	x	x	137, 142, 143, 154
Plastic and the environment	x	x	32, 37, 55, 59
Cities, communities, and modern life	x	x	121, 132, 137
Sports and performance	x	x	159, 164, 165
Businesses and the economy	x	x	44, 76, 77, 88
The impact of art and photographs	x	x	5, 10, 15
Food	x		49, 54
Inventions	x	x	59, 66
Laughter and humor	x		110
Improving your life	x		15
Feelings	x		5

CREDITS

Illustrations: All illustrations are owned by © Cengage.

Cover © Kent Shiraishi; **2–3** (spread) Charlie Hamilton James/National Geographic Image Collection; **4** © Marc Henauer; **6–7** (spread) © Joel Sartore/National Geographic Image Collection; **8** Ruben Salgado Escudero/National Geographic Image Collection; **10** (c) © Mark Bridger, (b) Tim Laman Photography/National Geographic Image Collection; **12–13** (spread) Ed Kashi/VII/Redux; **17** Onny Carr/Moment/Getty Images; **19** Dave Williams/Moment/Getty Images; **21** NurPhoto/Getty Images; **24–25** (spread) David Ramos/Getty Images News/Getty Images; **26** Sebastian Condrea/Moment/Getty Images; **28–29** (spread) Luca Locatelli/National Geographic Image Collection; **30** Luca Locatelli/National Geographic Image Collection; **34–35** (spread) Roman Sigaev/Alamy Stock Photo; **36** AP Images/picture-alliance/dpa/Daniel Karmann; **38** Santiago Urquijo/Moment/Getty Images; **40** Jonathan Nackstrand/AFP/Getty Images; **46–47** (spread) Universal History Archive/Universal Images Group/Getty Images; **48** Junko Kimura/Getty Images News/Getty Images; **50–51** (spread) Du Yubao Xinhua/eyevine/Redux; **52** NASA; **54** Daniel Schoenen/image Broker/Alamy Stock Photo; **56–57** (spread) Fred Marvaux/REA/Redux; **59** Matt Cardy/Getty Images News/Getty Images; **60** FPG/Archive Photos/Getty Images; **63** Science & Society Picture Library/SSPL/Getty Images; **68–69** (spread) Ciril Jazbec/National Geographic Image Collection; **70** mariakray/Shutterstock.com; **72–73** (spread) Eric Martin/Figarophoto/Redux; **74** John Coletti/Jon Arnold Images Ltd/Alamy Stock Photo; **78** © Shiok Meats; **78–79** (spread) © Shiok Meats; **83** S Bardens - British Athletics/British Athletics/Getty Images; **86** Emmanuel Dunand/AFP/Getty Images; **90–91** (spread) Malcolm Fairman/Alamy Stock Photo; **92** Barry Bland/Shutterstock.com; **94–95** (spread) Thought Catalog/Unsplash.com; **96** Eric Lafforgue/Art in All of Us/Corbis News/Getty Images; **100–101** (spread) Newsha Tavakolian/Magnum Photos; **106** Jonas Bendiksen/Magnum Photos; **110** David Gray/Reuters/Alamy Stock Photo; **112–113** (spread) Ayhan Altun/Moment/Getty Images; **114** © Daniel Raven-Ellison; **116–117** (spread) Luke Massey/MInden Pictures; **118** Xinhua News Agency/Getty Images; **122–123** (spread) © Spencer Lowell/Trunk Archive; **126** Faraway Photos/Alamy Stock Photo; **131** © Foundation Institute for Urban Development of the Republic of Tatarstan; **136** James Warwick/The Image Bank Unreleased/Getty Images; **140** Kisler Creations/Alamy Stock Photo; **146** AP Images/Gregory Bull; **148** Eye Ubiquitous/Universal Images Group/Getty Images; **152** © JenJenK http://devourtheworld.com; **134–135** (spread) © Murad Osmann; **138–139** (spread) © Cypress Peak Productions; **144–145** (spread) Barcroft Media/Getty Images; **156–157** (spread) Tiziana Fabi/AFP/Getty Images; **158** Dimitar Dilkoff/AFP/Getty Images; **160–161** (spread) Tony Karumba/AFP/Getty Images; **162** Gabriel Bouys/AFP/Getty Images; **164** Jono Searle - CA/Cricket Australia/Getty Images; **166–167** (spread) Luc Claessen/Velo/Getty Images; **170** Patrick Smith/Getty Images Sport/Getty Images.